Simple Psalter

for Solemnities, Feasts, and Other Celebrations

J. Michael Joncas

LITURGICAL PRESS
Collegeville, Minnesota

www.litpress.org

ACKNOWLEDGMENTS

Cover design: Tara Wiese. Photo courtesy of Getty Images.

ISBN: 978-0-8146-6745-3 ISBN: 978-0-8146-6746-0 (e-book)

Contents

Composer's Notes

My "simple psalms" project is intended to help worshiping communities with limited musical resources to sing the appointed Responsorial Psalm for the Sundays and Holydays of the Liturgical Year. I have set the texts as they appear in the English-language *Lectionary for Mass, Second Typical Edition* (1998) (antiphons) and the *Abbey Psalms and Canticles* (verses). All of the antiphons are set metrically (i.e., not in the free rhythm of chant) because I believe that in most cases in the English-speaking world this makes their texts more memorable and easier to sing for the assembly. The verses are set to rhythmic psalm-tones similar to those of Gelineau psalmody (i.e., speech-rhythm settings of the text over pulsed accompaniment ["sprung rhythm"]). Unlike the published Gelineau psalms, however, I have notated the way I propose that the texts to be sung since I find that it is sometimes difficult for cantors to sing the Gelineau tones as notated using only whole notes. A suggested tempo appears at the beginning of each psalm as a metronome mark; this tempo can be adjusted depending on the acoustic properties of the space in which the liturgy is celebrated.

Tones are assigned to each psalm based on the genre (*Gattung*) of the psalm-text, following the pattern of my friend and colleague, Art Zannoni, as follows:

Tone 1A: Hymn of Praise, Motivation from Nature
Tone 1B: Hymn of Praise from History or Torah
Tone 1C: Song of Zion
Tone 1D: Processional
Tone 1E: Hymn of Praise to YHWH as King
Tone 2A: Coronations or Anniversaries
Tone 2C: Royal Davidic Song of Thanksgiving
Tone 2D: Royal Davidic Marriage
Tone 3: Prophetic Psalms
Tone 4A: Community Lament
Tone 4B: Individual Lament
Tone 4C: Prayers for the Sick
Tone 5A: Communal Thanksgiving
Tone 5B: Individual Thanksgiving
Tone 6: Psalm of Confidence
Tone 8A: Wisdom Psalm 1
Tone 8B: Wisdom Psalm 2

(Missing tone numbers indicate a psalm-genre that does not appear in the Sunday and Solemnity Lectionary.)

I would here like to acknowledge the influence of three church composers whose psalm settings have influenced this project. I have already mentioned Fr. Joseph Gelineau, S.J., whose groundbreaking creation of "pulsed" psalm-tones set to sprung-rhythm texts made one of the metrical characteristics of Hebrew biblical psalms and canticles available for vernacular singing. A second influence was Howard Hughes, S.M., whose assigning of particular tones to particular genres of psalms based in contemporary form-critical analysis of the psalm-texts, has been eye- and ear-opening for me. Finally Paul Inwood was the first to call my attention to the idea of "psalm tunes" (rather than "psalm tones"). He showed how many English-language folk songs adjusted the fundamental melodic curves of their tones, eliding some syllables while assigning multiple notes to a single syllable based on the number of syllables needed.

Following the practice articulated in the *Lectionary for Mass*, these Responsorial Psalms would be performed as follows. After a period of silence to reflect on the previous scriptural reading proclaimed, a keyboard (or melody instrument) would play the melody for the Antiphon alone. The cantor would immediately intone the Antiphon with a keyboard providing accompaniment, if needed. The assembly would then repeat the Antiphon with a keyboard (and optionally other instruments) providing accompaniment, if needed. The cantor would then sing the assigned psalm verses with the assembly repeating the Antiphon after each verse.

While I believe these "simple psalms" can effectively be sung *a cappella* or with simple keyboard accompaniment, some communities might want to enhance their singing of the Responsorial Psalm with more elaborate music.

The optional harmony additions to the antiphons can be performed in a multitude of ways.

Vocally, the harmonies:

1) might be sung by soloists with the rest of the choir singing the antiphon in unison with the assembly.
2) might be sung by the soprano and alto sections of the choir with the men singing the antiphon in unison with the assembly.
3) If an SATB texture is desired, the soprano and bass sections sing the antiphon in unison with the assembly, with the tenors singing the higher harmonies an octave lower than written and the altos singing the lower harmonies as notated.

Instrumentally,

1) the SA harmonies might be played by C treble wind or string instruments, either as notated or an octave higher depending on where it best fits the instruments' tessitura.
2) the keyboardist should keep the pulse constant under the singing of the verses, but might repeat the chords as quarter notes rather than half notes, or even arpeggiate the chords as eighth notes if desired.

My preference is that the Verses be sung by a solo cantorial voice since that seems to ensure that the psalm-text be clearly sung and understood. Most of the time I have set the psalm-text for two phrases on one breath; the cantor should feel free to take a breath at an appropriate place if singing both phrases on one breath is too taxing. It is also possible to alternate male and female solo voices on the Verses, possibly with both singing the final Verse in octaves. It would also be possible to have the choir sing the verses (or just the final Verse) in unison, as long as their articulation keeps the psalm-text intelligible.

As the *Lectionary for Mass* reminds us: "The working of the Holy Spirit is needed if the word of God is to make what we hear outwardly have its effect inwardly. Because of the Holy Spirit's inspiration and support, the word of God becomes the foundation of the liturgical celebration and the rule and support of all our life. The working of the Holy Spirit precedes, accompanies and brings to completion the whole celebration of the Liturgy. But the Spirit also brings home to each person individually everything that in the proclamation of the word of God is spoken for the good of the whole gathering of the faithful" [9]. I pray that my musical settings of these "simple psalms" may help Christ's faithful, individually and collectively, hear the word of God and put it into practice in their lives. *Soli Deo gloria*.

(Fr. Jan) Michael Joncas
St. Paul, MN

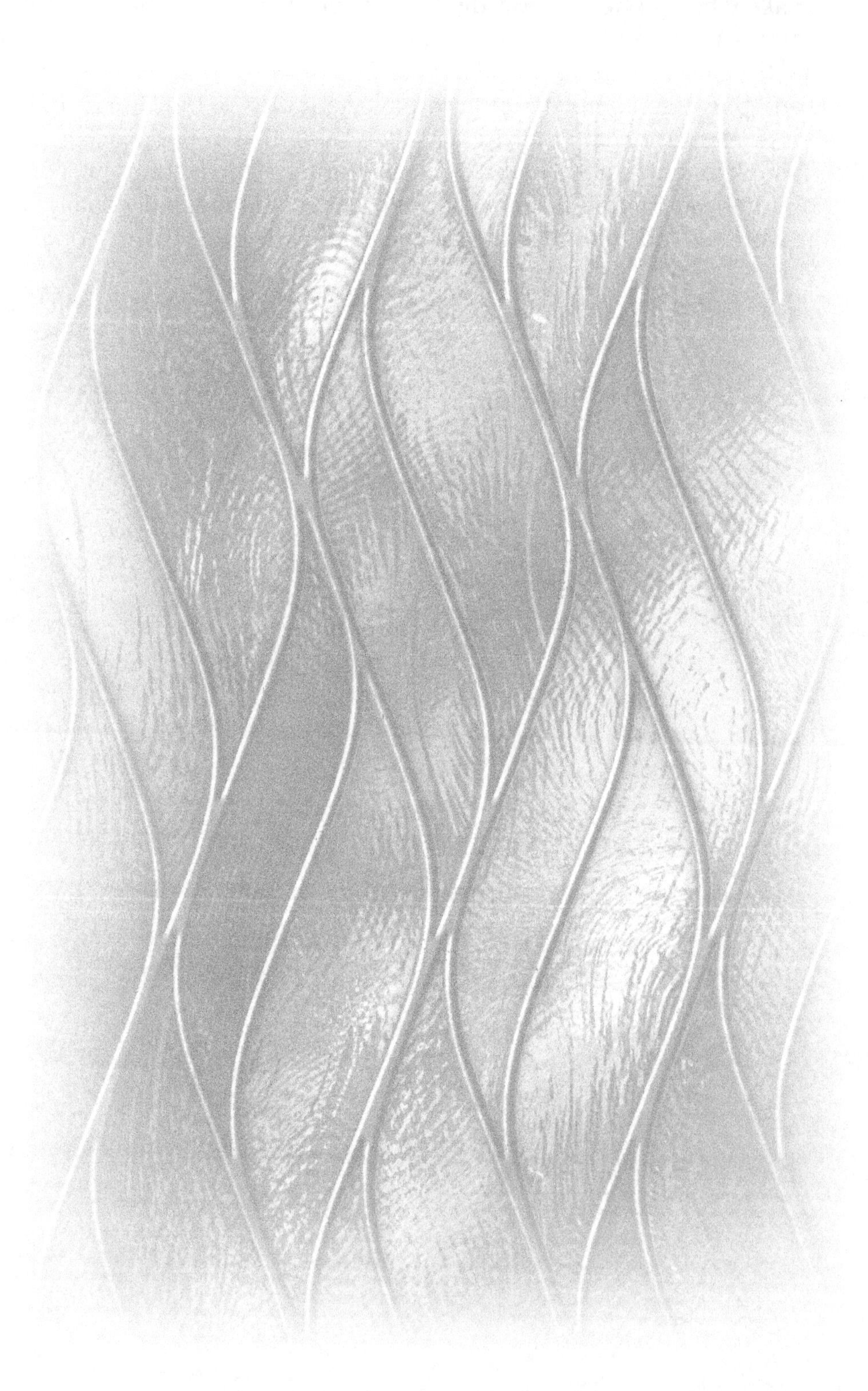

Psalm 89: For Ever I Will Sing

The Nativity of the Lord (Christmas): Vigil Mass

Psalm 89:4-5, 16-17, 27, 29

Michael Joncas
Tone 1E: Hymn of Praise to YHWH as King

With confidence ♩ = 80
Antiphon
Harmony
For ev - er I will sing the good - ness of the Lord.
Melody
For ev - er I___ will sing the good - ness of the Lord.
G C G D Em Am7 DSUS4 D G
Verse 1
1. "With my cho - sen one I have made a co - ve - nant; I have sworn to Da - vid my
G Am7 D Em Em7 Am7 D
ser - vant: I will es - tab - lish your des - cen - dants for - ev - er,
G D D7 G C A D

The Nativity of the Lord (Christmas): Vigil Mass

13
and set up your throne through all a - ges."
D7 Em D G D
Verse 2
17
2. How bless-ed the peo-ple who know your praise, who walk, O LORD, in the
G Am7 D Em Em7 Am7 D
21
light of your face, who find their joy ev'-ry day in your name,
G D D7 G C A D
25
who make your up-right-ness their joy-ful ac-claim.
D7 Em D G D

The Nativity of the Lord (Christmas): Vigil Mass

Verse 3
29
3. "He will call out to me, 'You are my fa - ther, my God, the rock of
G Am7 D Em Em7 Am7 D
33
my sal - va - tion.' I will keep my faith - ful love for him al - ways,
G D D7 G C A D
37
with him my co - ve - nant shall last."
D7 Em D G D

Psalm 96: Today Is Born Our Savior

The Nativity of the Lord (Christmas): Mass during the Night

Psalm 96:1-2, 2-3, 11-12, 13

Michael Joncas
Tone 1E: Hymn of Praise
to YHWH as King

With joy ♩ = 80
Antiphon
Harmony
To - day is born our Sa - vior, our Sa - vior, Christ the Lord.
Melody
To - day is born our Sa - vior, our Sa - vior, Christ the Lord.
G C G D Em Am Dsus4 D G
Verse 1
1. O sing a new song to the Lord; sing to the Lord,
G Am7 D Em Em7 G C
all the earth. O sing to the Lord; bless his name.
A D D7 Em D G D

The Nativity of the Lord (Christmas): Mass during the Night

Verse 2
14
2. Pro - claim his sal - va - tion day by day. Tell a - mong the na - tions his
G Am7 D Em Em7 G C
18
glo - ry, and his won - ders a - mong all the peo - ples.
A D D7 Em D G D
Verse 3
23
3. Let the hea-vens re-joice and earth be glad; let the sea and all with - in it
G Am7 D Em Em7 Am7 D

The Nativity of the Lord (Christmas): Mass during the Night

27
thun - der praise. Let the field and all it bears ex - ult.
G D D7 G C A D
29
Then will all the trees of the wood shout for joy.
D7 Em D G D
Verse 4
33
4. They will shout at the pre-sence of the Lord, for he comes, he comes to
G Am7 D Em Em7 Am7 D

The Nativity of the Lord (Christmas): Mass during the Night

36
judge the earth. He will judge the world with jus - tice,
G D D7 G C A D
and the peo - ples with faith - ful - ness.
D7 Em D G D

Psalm 97: A Light Will Shine

The Nativity of the Lord (Christmas): Mass at Dawn

Psalm 97:1, 6, 11-12

Michael Joncas
Tone 1E: Hymn of Praise
to YHWH as King

With confidence ♩ = 80
Antiphon
Harmony
A light will shine on us this day: the Lord is born for ___ us.
Melody
A light will shine on ___ us this day: the Lord is ___ born for us.
G C G D Em Am7 DSUS4 D G
Verse 1
1. The LORD is king, let earth re - joice; let the ma - ny is - lands be glad.
3
G Am7 G Em Em7 Am D7 G D

Text: Refrain, *Lectionary for the Mass*, © 1969, 1997, ICEL; Verses, *The Abbey Psalms and Canticles*,
© 2018, 2010, United States Conference of Catholic Bishops, Washington, DC. All rights reserved.
Music: Copyright © 2022 The Jan Michael Joncas Trust.
Published and administered by Liturgical Press, Collegeville, MN 56321. All rights reserved.

The Nativity of the Lord (Christmas): Mass at Dawn

11
The skies pro-claim his jus - tice; all peo - ples see his glo - ry.
D7 G C A D D7 Em D G D
Verse 2
18
2. Light shines forth for the just one, and joy for the up-right of heart. Re -
G Am7 G Em Em7 Am D7 G D D7
24
joice in the LORD, all you just, to the mem'-ry of his ho-li-ness give thanks.
G C A D D7 Em D G D

Psalm 98: All the Ends of the Earth

The Nativity of the Lord (Christmas): Mass during the Day

Psalm 98:1, 2-3ab, 3bc-4, 5-6

Michael Joncas
Tone 1E: Hymn of Praise to YHWH as King

With confidence ♩ = 80
Antiphon
Harmony
All the ends of the earth have seen the sav - ing power of God.
Melody
All the ends of the earth have seen the sav - ing power of God.
G C G D Em Am7 DSUS4 D G
Verse 1
1. O sing a new song to the LORD, for he has worked won - ders.
G C D Em Em7 C D G D
His right hand and his ho - ly arm have brought sal - va - tion.
D7 G C A D D7 Em D G D

The Nativity of the Lord (Christmas): Mass during the Day

Verse 2
17
2. The LORD has made known his sal-va-tion, has shown his de-liv'-rance to the na-tions. He has re-
G C D Em Em7 C D G D D7
23
mem - bered his mer-ci-ful love and his truth for the house of Is-ra-el.
G C A D D7 Em D G D
Verse 3
29
3. All the ends of the earth have seen, have seen the sal-va-tion of our God.
G C D Em Em7 C D G D D7

The Nativity of the Lord (Christmas): Mass during the Day

35
Shout to the LORD, all the earth; break forth in-to joy-ous song, and sing out your praise.
G C A D D7 Em D G D
Verse 4
41
4. Sing psalms to the LORD with the harp, with the harp and the sound of song. With
G C D Em Em7 C D G D D7
47
trum-pets and the sound of the horn, raise a shout be-fore the King, the LORD.
G C A D D7 Em D G D

Psalm 67: May God Bless Us

Solemnity of Mary, the Holy Mother of God

Psalm 67:2-3, 5, 6, 8

Michael Joncas
Tone 5A: Communal Thanksgiving

With gladness ♩ = 100
Antiphon
Harmony
May God bless us, bless us in his mer - cy.
Melody
May God bless us, bless us in his mer - cy.
D Em/D Bm Em G/A D
Verse 1
1. May God be gra - cious and bless us and let his face shed its
D Dmaj7 G/D D D/C♯ G Em7
light up - on us. So will your ways be known up on earth
D A A/G D G F♯ Bm

Solemnity of Mary, the Holy Mother of God

13
and all na - tions learn your sal - va - tion.
Bm/A G Em A SUS4
Verse 2
17
2. Let the na-tions be glad and shout for joy; with up - right-ness you rule the
D Dmaj7 G D D/C♯ G Em
21
peo - ples, you guide the na-tions on earth.
D A A/G G Em A SUS4 A

Solemnity of Mary, the Holy Mother of God

Verse 3
26
3. Let the peo - ples praise you, O God; let all the peo - ples
D Dmaj7 G/D D D/C♯ G Em7
30
praise you. May God still give us his bless - ing
D A A/G D G F♯ Bm
34
that all the ends of the earth may re - vere him.
Bm/A G Em ASUS4

Psalm 72: Lord, Every Nation

The Epiphany of the Lord

Psalm 72:1-2, 7-8, 10-11, 12-13

Michael Joncas
Tone 2A: Coronations and Anniversaries

With joy ♩. = 50
Antiphon
Harmony
Lord, ev' - ry na - tion on earth will a - dore you;
Melody
Lord, ev' - ry na - tion on earth will a - dore you;
Capo 3: G Am7 Bm Em Am7 G DSUS4 D7
B♭ Cm7 Dm Gm Cm7 B♭ FSUS4 F7
5
Lord, ev - 'ry na-tion on earth will a - dore you
Lord, ev' - ry na - tion on earth will a - dore you.
G Am7 Bm Em C D GSUS4 G GSUS4 G
B♭ Cm7 Dm Gm E♭ F B♭SUS4 B♭ B♭SUS4 B♭

Verse 1
1. O God, give your judg-ment to the king, to a king's son your jus-tice, that he may
G C Am7 DSUS4 D
B♭ E♭ Cm7 FSUS4 F
judge your peo-ple in jus-tice, and your poor in right judg - ment.
Em D C Am7 DSUS4 D DSUS4 D
Gm F E♭ Cm7 FSUS4 F FSUS4 F
Verse 2
2. In his days jus - tice shall flou-rish, and great peace till the moon is no more. He shall
G C Am7 DSUS4 D
B♭ E♭ Cm7 FSUS4 F

The Epiphany of the Lord

23
rule from sea to sea, from the Ri - ver to the bounds of the earth.
Em D C Am7 DSUS4 D DSUS4 D
Gm F E♭ Cm7 FSUS4 F FSUS4 F
Verse 3
28
3. The kings of Tar - shish and the is - lands shall pay him
G C Am7
B♭ E♭ Cm7
31
tri - bute, the kings of She - ba and Se - ba shall bring him gifts. Be - fore him all kings shall fall
D D7 G Gmaj7 Am7 D7 Em D
F F7 B♭ B♭maj7 Cm7 F7 Gm F

The Epiphany of the Lord

35
pros - trate, all na - tions shall serve him.
C Am7 DSUS4 D DSUS4 D
E♭ Cm7 FSUS4 F FSUS4 F
Verse 4
39
4. For he will res - cue the need - y when they cry, the poor who have no one to
G C Am7
B♭ E♭ Cm7
42
help. He will have pi - ty on the weak and the need - y, and
DSUS4 D Em D C
FSUS4 F Gm F E♭
45
save the lives of the need - y.
Am7 DSUS4 D DSUS4 D
Cm7 FSUS4 F FSUS4 F

Psalm 51: Be Merciful, O Lord

Ash Wednesday

Psalm 51:3-4, 5-6, 12-13, 17

Michael Joncas
Tone 4B: Individual Lament

With contrition ♩ = 75
Antiphon
Harmony
Be mer-ci-ful, be mer-ci-ful, mer-ci-ful, O Lord, for we have sinned.
Melody
Be mer-ci-ful, O Lord, for we have sinned; be mer-ci-ful, O Lord, for we have sinned.
Capo 1: Em Am C G Am G Bm7 Em
Fm B♭m D♭ A♭ B♭m A♭ Cm7 Fm
Verse 1
6
1. Have mer-cy on me, O God, ac - cord-ing to your mer-ci-ful love; ac -
Em7 Am/G Em7 AmSUS2 Em7 AmSUS2
Fm7 B♭m/A♭ Fm7 B♭mSUS2 Fm7 B♭mSUS2

Ash Wednesday

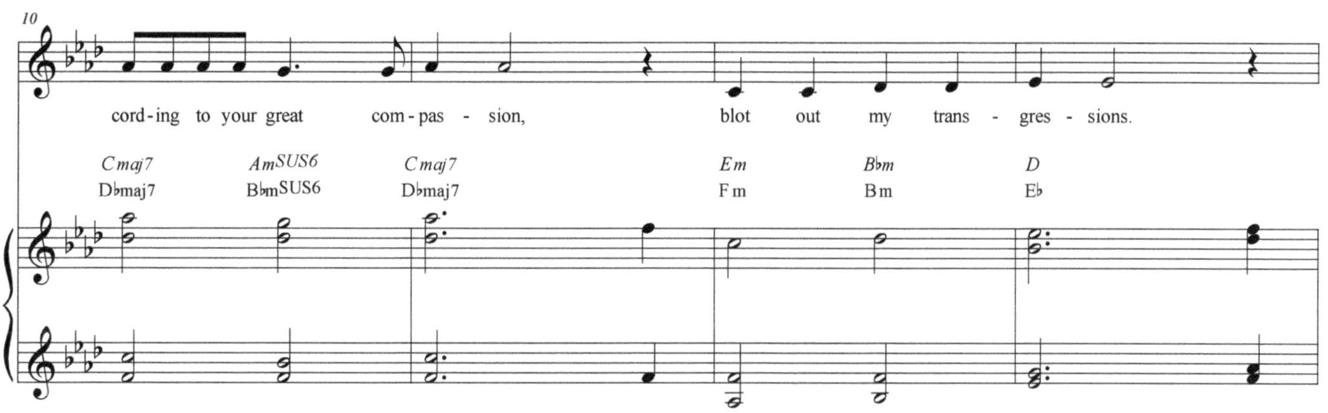
10
cord-ing to your great com-pas - sion, blot out my trans - gres - sions.
Cmaj7 AmSUS6 Cmaj7 Em B♭m D
D♭maj7 B♭mSUS6 D♭maj7 Fm Bm E♭

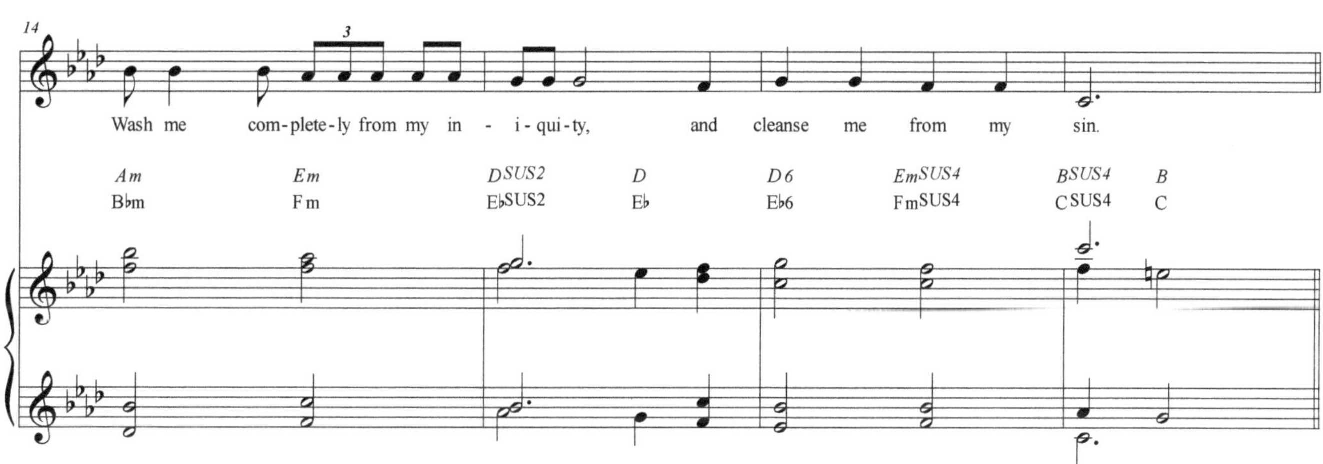
14
3
Wash me com-plete-ly from my in - i-qui-ty, and cleanse me from my sin.
Am Em DSUS2 D D6 EmSUS4 BSUS4 B
B♭m Fm E♭SUS2 E♭ E♭6 FmSUS4 CSUS4 C

Verse 2
18
3
2. My trans - gres - sions, tru - ly I know them; my sin is al-ways be - fore me. A-gainst
Em7 Am/G Em7 AmSUS2 Em7 AmSUS2
Fm7 B♭m/A♭ Fm7 B♭mSUS2 Fm7 B♭mSUS2

22
you, you a - lone have I sinned; what is e - vil in your sight I have done.
Cmaj7 AmSUS6 Cmaj7 D6 EmSUS4 BSUS4 B
D♭maj7 B♭mSUS6 D♭maj7 E♭6 FmSUS4 CSUS4 C

Verse 3
26
3. Cre - ate a pure heart for me, O God; re-new a stead - fast spi-rit with - in me. Do not
Em7 Am/G Em7 AmSUS2 Em7 AmSUS2
Fm7 B♭m/A♭ Fm7 B♭mSUS2 Fm7 B♭mSUS2

30
cast me a - way from your pre - sence; take not your ho - ly spi - rit from me.
Cmaj7 AmSUS6 Cmaj7 D6 EmSUS4 BSUS4 B
D♭maj7 B♭mSUS6 D♭maj7 E♭6 FmSUS4 CSUS4 C

Ash Wednesday

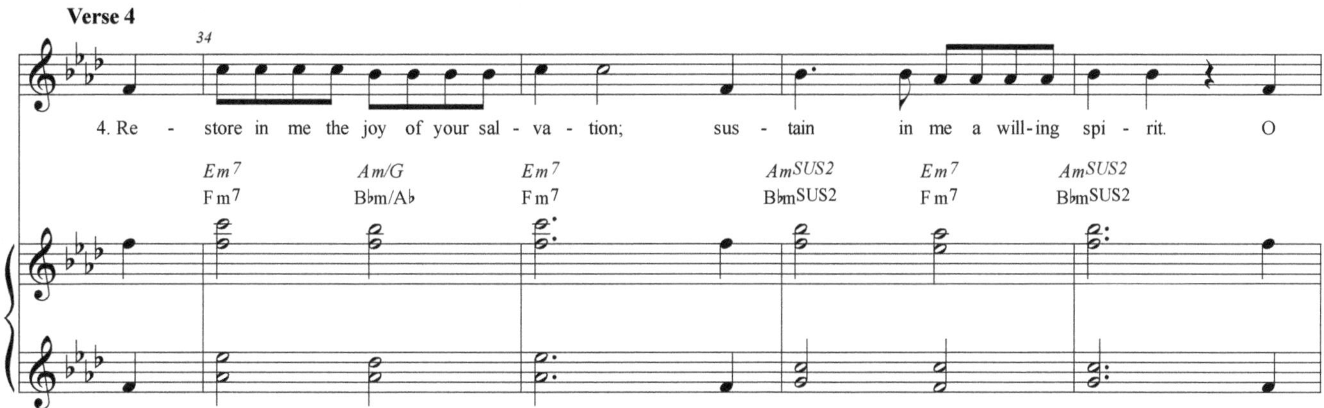
Verse 4
34
4. Re - store in me the joy of your sal - va - tion; sus - tain in me a will-ing spi - rit. O
Em7 Am/G Em7 AmSUS2 Em7 AmSUS2
Fm7 B♭m/A♭ Fm7 B♭mSUS2 Fm7 B♭mSUS2

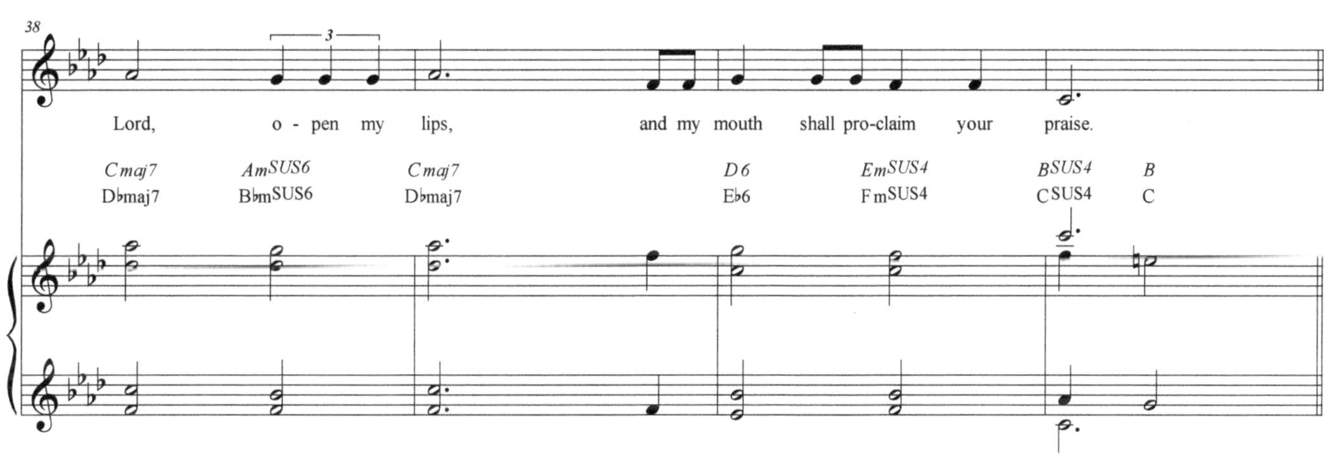
38
3
Lord, o - pen my lips, and my mouth shall pro-claim your praise.
Cmaj7 AmSUS6 Cmaj7 D6 EmSUS4 BSUS4 B
D♭maj7 B♭mSUS6 D♭maj7 E♭6 FmSUS4 CSUS4 C

Psalm 22: My God, My God, Why Have You Abandoned Me?

Palm Sunday of the Lord's Passion

Psalm 22:8-9, 17-18, 19-20, 23-24

Michael Joncas
Tone 4B: Individual Lament

With intensity ♩ = 75
Antiphon
Harmony
My God, my God, why have you a - ban - doned me?
Melody
My God, my God, why have you a - ban - doned me?
Capo 1: AmSUS4 Am GSUS4 G Am AmSUS2 Bm7 EmSUS4 Em EmSUS4 Em
B♭mSUS4 B♭m A♭SUS4 A♭ B♭m B♭mSUS2 Cm7 FmSUS4 Fm FmSUS4 Fm
Verse 1
1. All who see me de - ride me; they curl their lips, they toss their heads: "He
Em7 Am/G Em7 AmSUS2 Em7 AmSUS2
Fm7 B♭m/A♭ Fm7 B♭mSUS2 Fm7 B♭mSUS2

Palm Sunday of the Lord's Passion

11
trust - ed in the LORD, let him save him; let him re - lease him, for in him he de - lights."
Cmaj7 AmSUS2 Cmaj7 D6 EmSUS4 BSUS4 B
D♭maj7 B♭mSUS2 D♭maj7 E♭6 FmSUS4 CSUS4 C
Verse 2
15
2. For dogs have sur - round-ed me; a band of the wick-ed be - sets me. They tear
Em7 Am/G Em7 AmSUS2 Em7 AmSUS2
Fm7 B♭m/A♭ Fm7 B♭mSUS2 Fm7 B♭mSUS2
19
holes in my hands and my feet; I can count ev' - ry one of my bones.
Cmaj7 AmSUS2 Cmaj7 D6 EmSUS4 BSUS4 B
D♭maj7 B♭mSUS2 D♭maj7 E♭6 FmSUS4 CSUS4 C

Palm Sunday of the Lord's Passion

Verse 3
23
3. They di - vide my clo - thing a - mong them, they cast lots for my robe. But you, O
Em7 Am/G Em7 AmSUS2 Em7 AmSUS2
Fm7 B♭m/A♭ Fm7 B♭mSUS2 Fm7 B♭mSUS2
27
Lord, do not stay a - far off; my strength, make haste to help me!
Cmaj7 AmSUS2 Cmaj7 D6 EmSUS4 BSUS4 B
D♭maj7 B♭mSUS2 D♭maj7 E♭6 FmSUS4 CSUS4 C
Verse 4
31
4. I will tell of your name to my kin, and praise you in the midst of the as - sem - bly.
Em7 Am/G Em7 AmSUS2 Em7 AmSUS2
Fm7 B♭m/A♭ Fm7 B♭mSUS2 Fm7 B♭mSUS2

Palm Sunday of the Lord's Passion

35
"You who fear the LORD, give him praise; all des - cen - dants of Ja - cob, give him glo - ry; re -
Cmaj7 AmSUS6 Cmaj7 Em/G Am D
D♭maj7 B♭mSUS6 D♭maj7 Fm/A♭ B♭m E♭
39
vere him, all you des - cen - dants of Is - ra - el."
Am Em DSUS2 D D6 EmSUS4 BSUS4 B
B♭m Fm E♭SUS2 E♭ E♭6 FmSUS4 CSUS4 C

Psalm 89: For Ever I Will Sing

Holy Thursday: Chrism Mass

Psalm 89:21-22, 25 and 27
Michael Joncas
Tone 1E: Hymn of Praise to YHWH as King
With confidence ♩ = 80
Antiphon
Harmony
For ev - er I will sing the good - ness of the Lord.
Melody
For ev - er I will sing the good - ness of the Lord.
G C G D Em Am DSUS4 D G
Verse 1
1. "I have found my ser - vant Da - vid, and with my ho - ly oil a - noint-ed him. My
G Am7 D/F# Em Em7 Am D G D D7
hand shall al - ways be with him, and my arm shall make him strong."
G C A/C# D D7 C D G/B D

Holy Thursday: Chrism Mass

Verse 2
2. "My mer - cy and my faith - ful - ness shall be with him; by my
G Am7 D/F♯ Em Em7
name his might shall be ex - alt - ed. He will call out to me, 'You are my fa - ther,
Am D G D D7 G C A/C♯ D
my God, the rock of my sal - va - tion.'"
D7 C D G/B D

Psalm 116: Our Blessing-Cup

Holy Thursday: Evening Mass of the Lord's Supper

Psalm 116:12-13, 15-16bc, 17-18

Michael Joncas
Tone 5B: Individual Thanksgiving

Thankfully ♩= 75
Antiphon
Harmony
Melody
Our blessing-cup is a communion with the Blood of Christ.
Our blessing-cup is a communion, a communion with the Blood of Christ.
D G A Bm D/F♯ Em D G A7 D
Verse 1
1. How can I repay the Lord for all his goodness to me? The
D D/C♯ DSUS2 D Em7 D/C♯ ASUS4 A
cup of salvation I will raise; I will call on the name of the Lord.
G F♯7 Bm D/A Em7 ASUS4 A

Holy Thursday: Evening Mass of the Lord's Supper

Verse 2
13
2. How pre - cious in the eyes of the Lord is the death of his
D D/C♯ DSUS2 D Em7 D/C♯
16
faith - ful. Your ser - vant, Lord, your ser - vant am I, the
ASUS4 A Em7 F♯7 Bm D/A
19
son of your hand - maid; you have loos - ened my bonds.
A E7 ASUS4 A Em7 ASUS4 A

Holy Thursday: Evening Mass of the Lord's Supper

Verse 3
3. I will of - fer you a thanks - giv - ing sac - ri - fice; I will call on the name of the
D D/C♯ DSUS2 D Em7 D/C♯
LORD. My vows to the LORD I will ful - fill be - fore all his peo - ple.
ASUS4 A G F♯7 Bm D/A Em7 ASUS4 A

Psalm 31: Father, Into Your Hands

Good Friday of the Lord's Passion

Psalm 31:2, 6, 12-13, 15-16, 17, 25

Michael Joncas
Tone 4C: Prayers for the Sick

Pleadingly ♩ = 70
Antiphon
Harmony
Melody
(Final)
Fa - ther, in - to your hands, in - to your hands I com-mend my spi - rit.
Capo 1: Em D Cmaj7 Bm7 Em
Fm E♭ D♭maj7 Cm7 Fm
Verse 1
1. In you, O LORD, I take re - fuge. Let me ne - ver be put to shame. In your
D/E Cmaj7/E EmSUS4 Em Am D G C
E♭/F D♭maj7/F FmSUS4 Fm B♭m E♭ A♭ D♭
jus - tice, set me free; In - to your hands I com - mend my
Am G DSUS4 D G6 Am
B♭m A♭ E♭SUS4 E♭ A♭6 B♭m

Good Friday of the Lord's Passion

13
spi - rit. You will re-deem me, O LORD, O faith - ful God.
Em C Am Em7 D Cmaj7 Bm7 EmSUS4 Em
Fm D♭ B♭m Fm7 E♭ D♭maj7 Cm7 FmSUS4 Fm
Verse 2
18
2. Be-cause of all my foes I have be-come a re - proach, an ob - ject of scorn to my
D/E Cmaj7/E EmSUS4 Em Am D
E♭/F D♭maj7/F FmSUS4 Fm B♭m E♭
22
neigh - bors and of fear to my friends. Those who see me in the street, they
G C Am G DSUS4 D G6 Am
A♭ D♭ B♭m A♭ E♭SUS4 E♭ A♭6 B♭m

Good Friday of the Lord's Passion

26
flee from me. I am for - got-ten like some - one dead, and have be - come like a bro - ken ves - sel.
Em C Am Em7 D Cmaj7 Bm7 EmSUS4 Em
Fm D♭ B♭m Fm7 E♭ D♭maj7 Cm7 FmSUS4 Fm
Verse 3
31
3. But as for me, I trust in you, O LORD; I say, "You are my
D/E Cmaj7/E EmSUS4 Em Am D
E♭/F D♭maj7/F FmSUS4 Fm B♭m E♭
35
God. There in your hands is my lot, from the
G C Am G DSUS4 D
A♭ D♭ B♭m A♭ E♭SUS4 E♭

Good Friday of the Lord's Passion

38
hands of my e - ne-mies de - li - ver me, and from those who pur - sue me."
G6 Am Em C Cmaj7/E Bm7 EmSUS4 Em
A♭6 B♭m Fm D♭ D♭maj7/F Cm7 FmSUS4 Fm
Verse 4
42
4." Let your face shine on your ser - vant. Save me in your mer - ci - ful
D/E Cmaj7/E EmSUS4 Em Am D
E♭/F D♭maj7/F FmSUS4 Fm B♭m E♭
46
love." Be strong; let your heart take cour - age, all who hope in the LORD.
G C Am G DSUS4 D Cmaj7/E Bm7 EmSUS4 Em
A♭ D♭ B♭m A♭ E♭SUS4 E♭ D♭maj7/F Cm7 FmSUS4 Fm

Psalm 104: Lord, Send Out Your Spirit

Holy Saturday at the Easter Vigil in the Holy Night 1A
Pentecost Sunday

Psalm 104:1-2, 5-6, 10, 12, 13-14, 24, 35

Michael Joncas
Tone 1A: Hymn of Praise
Motivation from Nature

In awe ♩ = 90
Antiphon
Harmony
Melody
Lord, send out your Spi - rit, LORD out
Lord, send out your Spi - rit, Lord, send out your Spi - rit,
C F GSUS4 G
Lord, send out your Spi - rit and re - new the face of the earth.
Lord, send out your Spi - rit and re - new the face of the earth.
C B♭ C B♭ C

Holy Saturday at the Easter Vigil in the Holy Night 1A
Pentecost Sunday

Verse 1
9
1. Bless the Lord, O my soul! O Lord, my God, how great you are,
C G Am Cmaj7 Dm7 Dm GSUS4 G
13
clothed in ma-jes-ty and ho-nor, wrapped in light as with a robe!
Am D C GSUS4 G
Verse 2
17
2. You set the earth on its foun-da-tion, im-mov-a-ble from age to age. You
C G Am Cmaj7 Dm7 Dm GSUS4 G
21
wrapped it with the depths like a cloak; the wa-ters stood high-er than the moun-tains.
Am D C GSUS4 G

Holy Saturday at the Easter Vigil in the Holy Night 1A
Pentecost Sunday

Verse 3
25
3. You make springs gush forth in the val - leys; they flow in be-tween the hills.
C G Am Cmaj7 Dm7 Dm GSUS4 G
29
There the birds of hea - ven build their nests; from the bran-ches they sing their song.
Am D C GSUS4 G
Verse 4
33
4. From your dwell-ing you wa - ter the moun - tains; by your works the earth has its
C G Am Cmaj7 Dm7 Dm
36
fill. You make the grass grow for the cat - tle and plants to serve man - kind's
GSUS4 G Am D G

Holy Saturday at the Easter Vigil in the Holy Night 1A
Pentecost Sunday

40
need, that he might bring forth bread from the earth.
C G C G SUS4 G
Verse 5
43
5. How ma - ny are your works, O LORD! In wis - dom you have made them
C G Am Cmaj7 Dm7 Dm
46
all. The earth is full of your crea - tures. Bless the LORD, O my soul!
G SUS4 G Am D C G SUS4 G

Psalm 33: The Earth Is Full of the Goodness of the Lord

Holy Saturday at the Easter Vigil in the Holy Night 1B

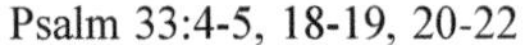

Psalm 33:4-5, 18-19, 20-22

Michael Joncas
Tone 1B: Hymn of Praise
from History or Torah

With awe ♩ = 80
Antiphon

Harmony
The earth is full of the good-ness of the Lord, of the good-ness of the Lord.
Melody
The earth is full of the good-ness of the Lord, of the good-ness of the Lord.
D G Gm D G C Am7 D
F B♭ B♭m F B♭ E♭ Cm7 F

Verse 1

1. The word of the LORD is up-right, and all his works to be trust-ed. The
D C/D Bm D Em D ASUS4 A
F E♭/F Dm F Gm F CSUS4 C

Holy Saturday at the Easter Vigil in the Holy Night 1B

10
LORD loves jus - tice and right, and his mer - ci - ful love fills the earth.
Am Cmaj7 DSUS2 D Am Am7 DSUS4 D
Cm E♭maj7 FSUS2 F Cm Cm7 FSUS4 F
Verse 2
14
2. By the word of the LORD the heav'ns were made, by the breath of his mouth all their host.
D C/D Bm D Em D ASUS4
F E♭/F Dm F Gm F CSUS4
18
As in a flask, he col-lects the waves of the o - cean; he stores up the depths of the sea.
A Am Cmaj7 DSUS2 D Am Am7 DSUS4 D
C Cm E♭maj7 FSUS2 F Cm Cm7 FSUS4 F

Holy Saturday at the Easter Vigil in the Holy Night 1B

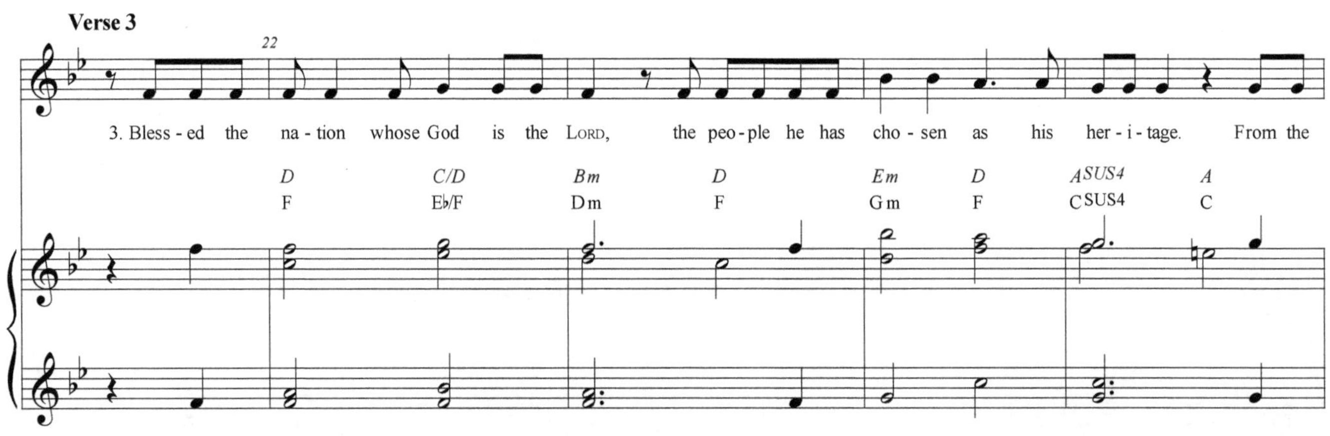
Verse 3
22
3. Bless - ed the na - tion whose God is the LORD, the peo - ple he has cho - sen as his her - i - tage. From the
D C/D Bm D Em D ASUS4 A
F E♭/F Dm F Gm F CSUS4 C

26
hea - vens the LORD looks forth; he sees the whole hu - man race.
Am Cmaj7 DSUS2 D Am Am7 DSUS4 D
Cm E♭maj7 FSUS2 F Cm Cm7 FSUS4 F

Verse 4
30
4. Our soul is wait - ing for the LORD. He is our help and our shield. May your
D C/D Bm D Em D ASUS4 A
F E♭/F Dm F Gm F CSUS4 C

Holy Saturday at the Easter Vigil in the Holy Night 1B

34
mer - ci - ful love be up - on us, as we hope in you, O LORD.
Am Cmaj7 DSUS2 D Am Am7 DSUS4 D
Cm E♭maj7 FSUS2 F Cm Cm7 FSUS4 F

Psalm 16: You Are My Inheritance

Holy Saturday at the Easter Vigil in the Holy Night 2

Psalm 16:5, 8, 9-10, 11

Michael Joncas
Tone 4C: Prayers for the Sick

With trust ♩ = 80
Antiphon
Harmony
You are my in - her - i - tance, my in - her - i - tance, O Lord.
Melody
You are my in - her - i - tance, O Lord.
Capo 1: Em Am D Bm7 EmSUS4 Em
Fm Bbm Eb Cm7 FmSUS4 Fm
Verse 1
5
1. O Lord, it is you who are my por-tion and cup; you your-self who se-cure my lot. I keep the
D/E C/E EmSUS4 Em Am D6 G C
Eb/F Db/F FmSUS4 Fm Bbm Eb6 Ab Db

Holy Saturday at the Easter Vigil in the Holy Night 2

9
LORD be-fore me al ways; with him at my right hand, I shall not be moved.
Am7 G DSUS4 D Em7 Am Em C Cmaj7 Bm7 EmSUS4 Em
B♭m7 A♭ E♭SUS4 E♭ Fm7 B♭m Fm D♭ D♭maj7 Cm7 FmSUS4 Fm
Verse 2
15
2. And so, my heart re-joi-ces, my soul is glad; e-ven my flesh shall rest in hope. For you will not a-
D/E C/E EmSUS4 Em Am D6 G C
E♭/F D♭/F FmSUS4 Fm B♭m E♭6 A♭ D♭
19
ban-don my soul to She - ol, nor let your ho-ly one see cor - rup-tion.
Am7 G DSUS4 D Cmaj7 Bm7 EmSUS4 E♭m
B♭m7 A♭ E♭SUS4 E♭ D♭maj7 Cm7 FmSUS4 Em

Holy Saturday at the Easter Vigil in the Holy Night 2

Verse 3
3. You will show me the path of life, the full - ness of joy in your
D/E C/E EmSUS4 Em Am D6
Eb/F Db/F FmSUS4 Fm Bbm Eb6
pre - sence, at your right hand, bliss for - ev - er.
G C Cmaj7 Bm7 EmSUS4 Ebm
Ab Db Dbmaj7 Cm7 FmSUS4 Em

Exodus 15: Let Us Sing to the Lord (Exodus Canticle)

Holy Saturday at the Easter Vigil in the Holy Night 3

Exodus 15:1-2, 3-4, 5-6, 17-18

Michael Joncas

With exultant praise ♩. = 50
Antiphon
Harmony
Melody
Let us sing to the Lord, sing to the Lord; he has co - vered him-self in glo-ry.
E F m7 Am E F♯m7 A E
Verse 1
1. Let us sing to the LORD who has glo - rious - ly tri - umphed; horse and ri - der he has
E F♯m7 B7 C♯mSUS4 C♯m A E F♯maj7
hurled in - to the sea. The LORD is my strength and might; he has be - come my sal -
E F♯m7 BSUS4 B E F♯m7 B7

Holy Saturday at the Easter Vigil in the Holy Night 3

16
va - tion. This is my God, and I will praise him, my fa - thers' God, and I will ex - alt him.
C♯mSUS4 C♯m A E F♯m7 C♯m7 F♯m7 B
Verse 2
21
2. The Lord is a war - rior; the LORD is his name. The cha - riots of Pha - roah and his ar - my he has
E F♯m7 B7 CmSUS4 C♯m
25
cast in - to the sea; the e - lite of his of - fi - cers were drowned in the Red Sea.
A B7 G♯m F♯7 E E6 C♯m7 B
Verse 3
31
3. The wa - ters of the flood co - vered o - ver them; they went down to the depths like a stone. Your right hand, O
E F♯m7 B7 C♯mSUS4 C♯m A B7

Holy Saturday at the Easter Vigil in the Holy Night 3

36
LORD, ma - jes - tic in power; your right hand, O LORD, shat - ters the en - e - my.
G♯m F♯m7 E E6 A D♯ F♯m7 C♯m7 B
Verse 4
43
4. You will bring them in and plant them up - on the mount of your in - her - i - tance: the
E F♯m7 B7 C♯mSUS4 C♯m
47
place which you, O LORD, have made your dwell - ing, the ho - ly place, O LORD that your
A B7 G♯m F♯m7 E E6
51
hands have es - tab - lished. The LORD will reign for - ev - er and ev - er.
A D♯ F♯m7 C♯m7 B

Psalm 30: I Will Praise You, Lord

Holy Saturday at the Easter Vigil in the Holy Night 4

Psalm 30:2, 4, 5-6, 11-12, 13

Michael Joncas
Tone 4C: Prayers for the Sick

In thanksgiving ♩ = 85
Antiphon
Harmony
Melody
I will praise you, you have res - cued me.
I will praise you, Lord, for you have res - cued me.
Capo 1: Em A Cmaj7 Bm7 ESUS4 E
Fm B♭ D♭maj7 Cm7 FSUS4 F

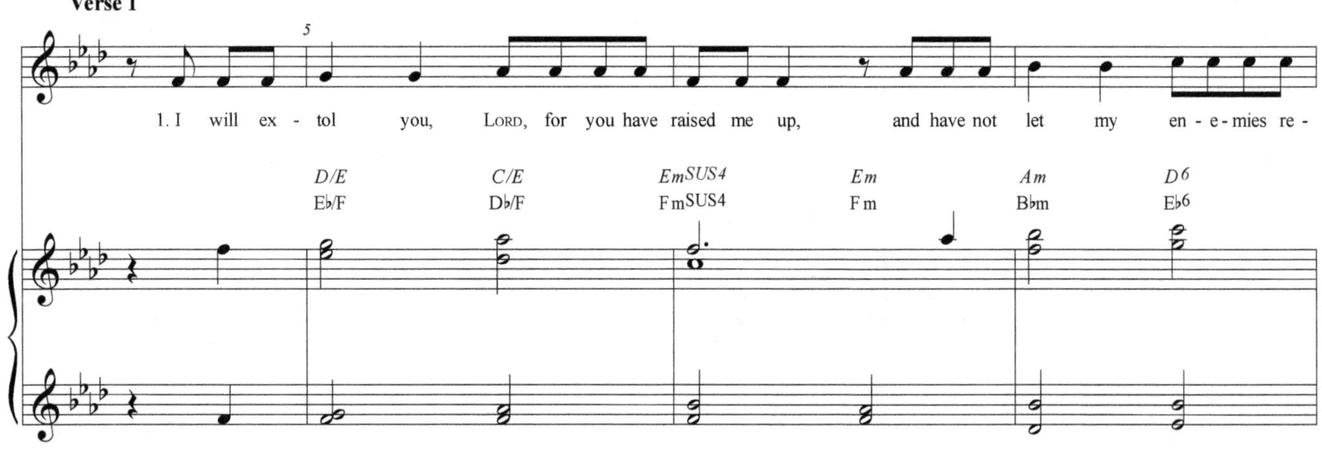

Verse 1
1. I will ex - tol you, Lord, for you have raised me up, and have not let my en - e - mies re -
D/E C/E EmSUS4 Em Am D6
E♭/F D♭/F FmSUS4 Fm B♭m E♭6

Holy Saturday at the Easter Vigil in the Holy Night 4

joice o - ver me. O LORD, you have lift - ed up my soul from She-ol, re - stored me to
G C Am7 G DSUS4 D Em7 Am
A♭ D♭ B♭m7 A♭ E♭SUS4 E♭ Fm7 B♭m
life from those who sink in - to the pit.
Em C Cmaj7 Bm7 EmSUS4 Em
Fm D♭ D♭maj7 Cm7 FmSUS4 Fm
Verse 2
2. Sing psalms to the LORD, you faith-ful ones; give thanks to his ho - ly name. His an - ger lasts a
D/E C/E EmSUS4 Em Am D6 G C Am7 G
E♭/F D♭/F FmSUS4 Fm B♭m E♭6 A♭ D♭ B♭m7 A♭

Holy Saturday at the Easter Vigil in the Holy Night 4

20
mo-ment; his fa - vor all through life. At night come tears, but dawn brings joy.
DSUS4 D Em7 Am Em C Am G D Cmaj7 Bm7 EmSUS4 Em
E♭SUS4 E♭ Fm7 B♭m Fm D♭ B♭m A♭ E♭ D♭maj7 Cm7 FmSUS4 Fm
Verse 3
27
3. Hear, O LORD, and have mer - cy on me; be my hel - per, O LORD. You have
D/E C/E EmSUS4 Em Am D6 G C
E♭/F D♭/F FmSUS4 Fm B♭m E♭6 A♭ D♭
31
changed my mourn-ing in-to danc-ing. O LORD, my God, I will thank you for - ev - er.
Am7 G DSUS4 D Em7 Am Em C Cmaj7 Bm7 EmSUS4 Em
B♭m7 A♭ E♭SUS4 E♭ Fm7 B♭m Fm D♭ D♭maj7 Cm7 FmSUS4 Fm

Isaiah 12: You Will Draw Water

Holy Saturday at the Easter Vigil in the Holy Night 5 and 7B
Sacred Heart of Jesus (B)

Isaiah 12:2-3, 4bcd, 5-6

Michael Joncas

With delight ♩. = 45
Antiphon
Harmony
You will draw wa-ter joy-ful-ly from the springs of sal-va-tion.
Melody
You will draw wa-ter joy-ful-ly from the springs of sal-va-tion.
C F C Am C G C
Verse 1
1. Be-hold, God is my sal-va-tion! I will trust and will not be a-fraid, for the
C G Am Am/G Dm7 F GSUS4 G
LORD is my strength and my praise, and he has been my sal-va-tion. With
Am Em DSUS2 D7 G F C G

Holy Saturday at the Easter Vigil in the Holy Night 5 and 7B
Sacred Heart of Jesus (B)

13
joy will you draw wa - ter___ from the springs of sal - va - tion.___
A A/G DmSUS2 Dm C Cmaj7 CSUS6 G
Verse 2
17
2. Give thanks to the LORD, in - voke his name; make known a-mong the peo - ples his
C G Am Am/G Am Em
20
deeds;___ pro - claim that his name is ex - alt - ed.___
DSUS2 D C Cmaj7 CSUS6 G

Holy Saturday at the Easter Vigil in the Holy Night 5 and 7B
Sacred Heart of Jesus (B)

Verse 3
3. Sing to the LORD for he has wrought won-ders; let this be known through all the earth.
C G Am Am/G F Cm7 GSUS4 G
Shout a - loud and sing praise, you who dwell in Zi - on, for
Am Em DSUS2 D7 G F C G
great in your midst is the Ho - ly One of Is - ra - el.
A A/G DmSUS2 Dm C Cmaj7 CSUS6 G

Psalm 19: Lord, You Have the Words

Holy Saturday at the Easter Vigil in the Holy Night 6

Psalm 19:8, 9, 10, 11
Michael Joncas
Tone 8B: Wisdom Psalm 2
Simply ♩ = 80
Antiphon
Harmony
Lord, you have the words of ev - er - last - ing life.
Melody
Lord, you have the words of ev - er last - ing life.
Capo 1: D G A D Bm Em/G D G A7 D
E♭ A♭ B♭ E♭ Cm Fm/A♭ E♭ A♭ B♭7 E♭
Verse 1
1. The law of the LORD is per - fect; it re-vives the soul. The de -
D6 G Em7 A D6 E7 ASUS4 A
E♭6 A♭ Fm7 B♭ E♭6 F7 B♭SUS4 B♭
crees of the LORD are stead - fast; they give wis - dom to the sim - ple.
Bm F♯m Gmaj7 Am/G Dmaj7 G ASUS4 A
Cm Gm A♭maj7 B♭m/A♭ E♭maj7 A♭ B♭SUS4 B♭

Verse 2
13
2. The pre-cepts of the LORD are right; they glad - den the heart. The com-
D6 G Em7 A D6 E7 ASUS4 A
E♭6 A♭ Fm7 B♭ E♭6 F7 B♭SUS4 B♭
17
mand of the LORD is clear; it gives light to the eyes.
Bm F♯m Gmaj7 Am/G Dmaj7 G ASUS4 A
Cm Gm A♭maj7 B♭m/A♭ E♭maj7 A♭ B♭SUS4 B♭
Verse 3
21
3. The fear of the LORD is pure, a - bid - ing for - ev - er. The
D6 G Em7 A D6 E7 ASUS4 A
E♭6 A♭ Fm7 B♭ E♭6 F7 B♭SUS4 B♭

Holy Saturday at the Easter Vigil in the Holy Night 6

25
judg - ments of the LORD are true; they are, all of them, just.
Bm F♯m Gmaj7 Am/G Dmaj7 G ASUS4 A
Cm Gm A♭maj7 B♭m/A♭ E♭maj7 A♭ B♭SUS4 B♭
Verse 4
29
4. They are more to be de-sired than gold, than quan - ti-ties of gold. And
D6 G Em7 A D6 E7 ASUS4 A
E♭6 A♭ Fm7 B♭ E♭6 F7 B♭SUS4 B♭
33
sweet - er are they than ho - ney, than ho - ney flow-ing from the comb.
Bm F♯m Gmaj7 Am/G Dmaj7 G ASUS4 A
Cm Gm A♭maj7 B♭m/A♭ E♭maj7 A♭ B♭SUS4 B♭

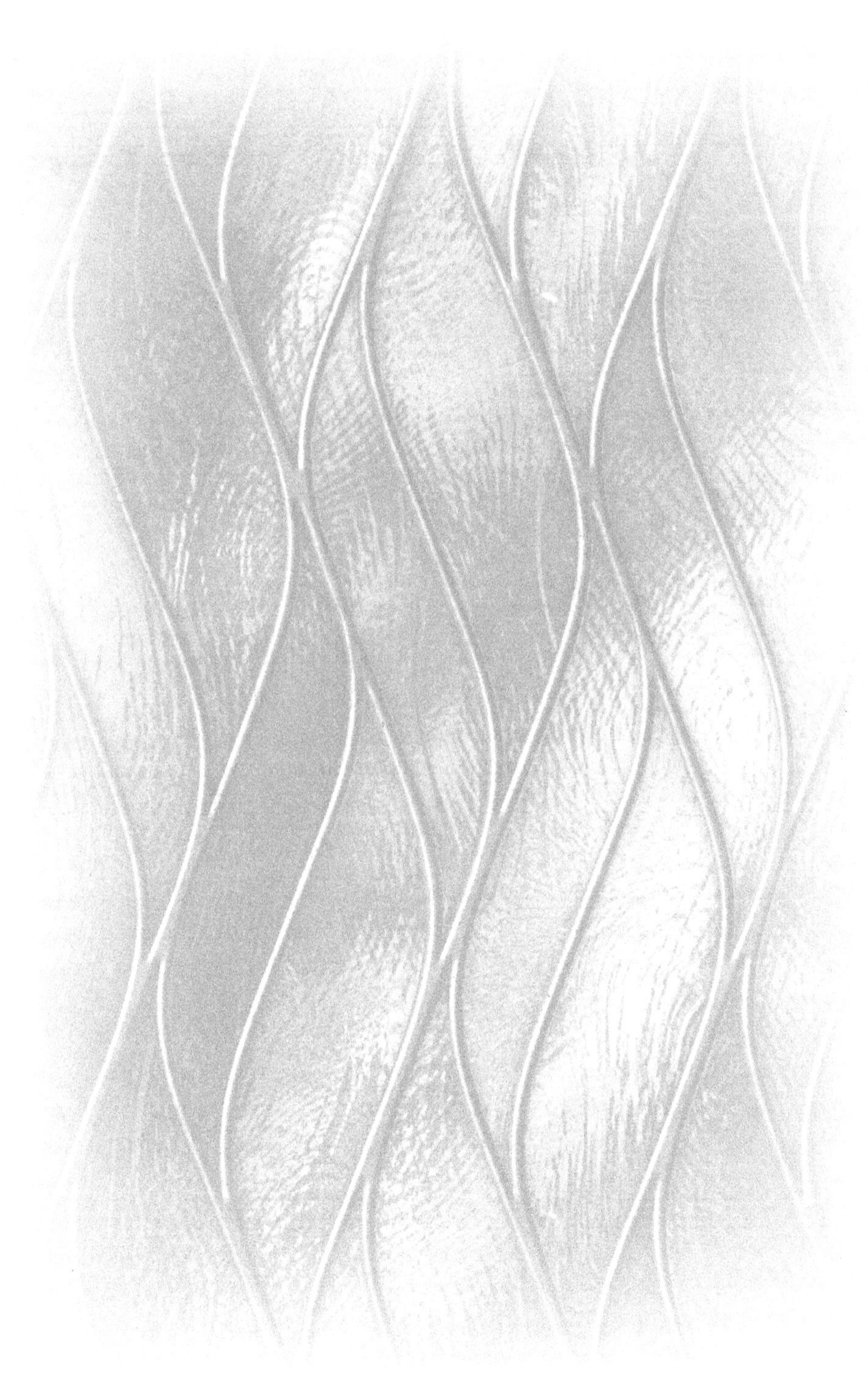

Psalm 42: Like a Deer*

Holy Saturday at the Easter Vigil in the Holy Night 7A

Psalm 42:3, 5; 43:3, 4

Michael Joncas
Tone 4B: Individual Laments

With confident pleading ♩ = 90

Antiphon

Harmony

Like a deer my soul longs for

Melody

Like a deer that longs for run - ing streams, my soul longs for

Capo 1: Em Em7 A A♯m Em Cmaj7

Fm Fm7 B♭ Bm Fm D♭maj7

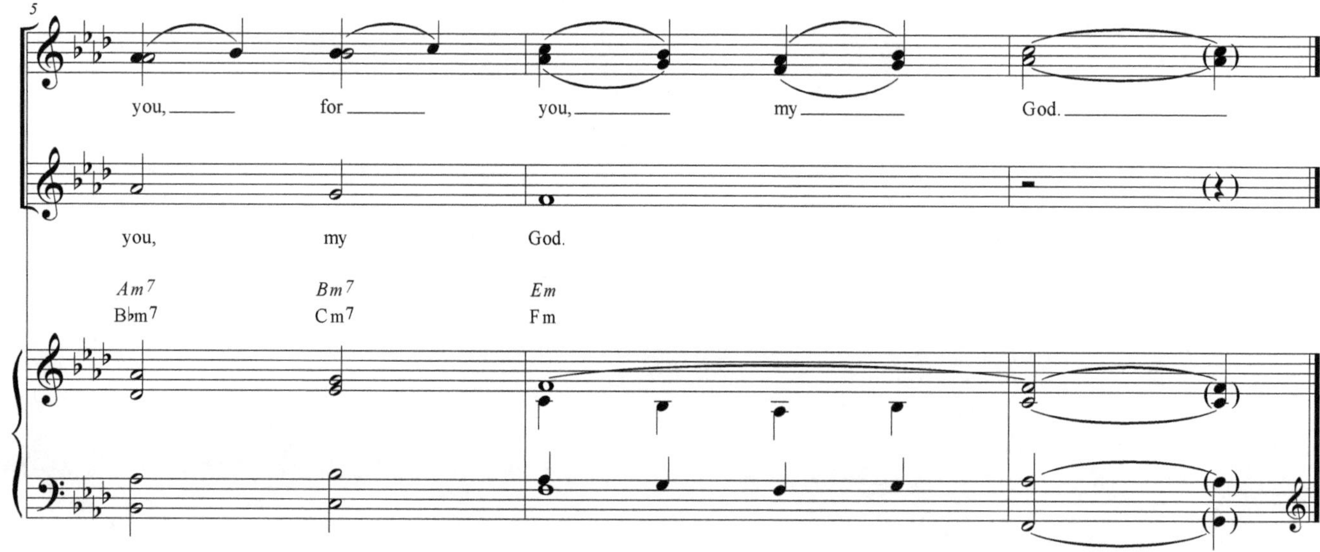

5
you, for you, my God.
you, my God.
Am7 Bm7 Em
B♭m7 Cm7 Fm

**Only used when baptism is celebrated.*

Holy Saturday at the Easter Vigil in the Holy Night 7A

Verse 1
8
1. My soul is thirs-ting for God, the liv - ing God;
Em7 Am/G Em7 AmSUS6 Em7 AmSUS2
Fm7 B♭m/A♭ Fm7 B♭mSUS6 Fm7 B♭mSUS2
12
when can I en-ter and ap-pear be - fore the face of God?
Cmaj7 AmSUS6 Cmaj7 D6 EmSUS4 BSUS4 B
D♭maj7 B♭mSUS6 D♭maj7 E♭6 FmSUS4 CSUS4 C
Verse 2
16
2. For I would go to the place of your won-drous tent, all the way to the house of God, a-mid
3
Em7 Am/G Em7 AmSUS6 Em7 AmSUS2
Fm7 B♭m/A♭ Fm7 B♭mSUS6 Fm7 B♭mSUS2

Holy Saturday at the Easter Vigil in the Holy Night 7A

20
cries of glad-ness and thanks-giv - ing, the throng keep-ing joy - ful fes - ti - val.
Cmaj7 AmSUS6 Cmaj7 D6 EmSUS4 BSUS4 B
D♭maj7 B♭mSUS6 D♭maj7 E♭6 FmSUS4 CSUS4 C
Verse 3
24
3. O send forth your light and your truth; they will guide me on. They will
Em7 Am/G Em7 AmSUS6 Em7 AmSUS2
Fm7 B♭m/A♭ Fm7 B♭mSUS6 Fm7 B♭mSUS2
28
bring me to your ho - ly moun - tain, to the place where you dwell.
Cmaj7 AmSUS6 Cmaj7 D6 EmSUS4 BSUS4 B
D♭maj7 B♭mSUS6 D♭maj7 E♭6 FmSUS4 CSUS4 C

Holy Saturday at the Easter Vigil in the Holy Night 7A

Verse 4
32
3
4. And I will come to the al - tar of God, to God, my joy and glad - ness. To
Em7 Am/G Em7 AmSUS6 Em7 AmSUS2
Fm7 B♭m/A♭ Fm7 B♭mSUS6 Fm7 B♭mSUS2

36

you will I give thanks on the harp, O God, my God!

Cmaj7 AmSUS6 Cmaj7 D6 EmSUS4 BSUS4 B

D♭maj7 B♭mSUS6 D♭maj7 E♭6 FmSUS4 CSUS4 C

Psalm 118: Alleluia!

Holy Saturday at the Easter Vigil in the Holy Night 8

Psalm 118:1-2, 16-17, 22-23

Michael Joncas
Tone 5A: Communal Thanksgiving

Joyfully ♩ = 80
Antiphon
Harmony
Al - le - lu - ia, Al - le - lu - ia, Al - le - lu - ia, Al - le - lu - ia.
Melody
Al - le - lu - ia, Al - le - lu - ia, Al - le - lu - ia, Al - le - lu - ia.
D Em7 A Bm Em7 D G A D
Verse 1
5
3
1. Give praise to the LORD, for he is good; his mercy endures for - ev - er.
D Dmaj7 G D D/C♯ G Em7 D A A7

Holy Saturday at the Easter Vigil in the Holy Night 8

11
Let the house of Is-ra-el say, "His mer-cy en-dures for-ev-er."
D G F♯ Bm Bm/A G Em ASUS4 A
Verse 2
18
2. "The LORD's right hand is ex-al-ted. The LORD's right hand has done migh-ty deeds."
D Dmaj7 G D D/C♯ G Em7 D A
23
I shall not die, I shall live and re-count the deeds of the LORD.
A7 D G F♯ Bm Bm/A G Em ASUS4 A

Holy Saturday at the Easter Vigil in the Holy Night 8

Verse 3
3. The stone that the build-ers re-ject-ed has be-come the cor-ner-stone.
D Dmaj7 G D D/C♯ G Em7 D A
By the LORD has this been done. a mar-vel in our eyes.
A7 D G F♯ Bm Bm/A G Em ASUS4 A

Psalm 118: This Is the Day

Easter Sunday: The Resurrection of the Lord

Psalm 118:1-2, 16-17, 22-23

Michael Joncas
Tone 5B: Individual Thanksgiving

Joyfully ♩ = 80
Antiphon
Harmony
Al - le - lu - ia, Al - le - lu - ia, Al - le - lu - ia, Al - le - lu - ia.
Melody
This is the day the Lord has made; let us re-joice, re - joice and be glad.
D Em7 A Bm Em7 D G A D
Alternate Antiphon
Al - le - lu - ia, Al - le - lu - ia, Al - le - lu - ia, Al - le - lu - ia.
Al - le - lu - ia, Al - le - lu - ia, Al - le - lu - ia, Al - le - lu - ia.
D Em7 A Bm Em7 D G A D

Easter Sunday: The Resurrection of the Lord

Verse 1
9
1. Give praise to the Lord for he is good; his mer-cy en-dures for - ev - er. Let the
D D/C♯ DSUS2 D Em7 Dmaj7 ASUS4 A
13
house of Is - ra - el say, "His mer - cy en - dures for - ev - er."
3
Em7 F♯7 Bm D Em7 ASUS4 A
Verse 2
17
2. "The Lord's right hand is ex - al - ted. The Lord's right hand has done migh - ty deeds."
D D/C♯ DSUS2 D Em7 Dmaj7 ASUS4 A

Easter Sunday: The Resurrection of the Lord

21
I shall not die, I shall live, and re - count the deeds of the LORD.
Em7 F♯7 Bm D Em7 ASUS4 A
Verse 3
25
3. The stone that the build - ers re - ject - ed has be - come the cor - ner - stone. By the
D D/C♯ DSUS2 D Em7 Dmaj7 ASUS4 A
29
LORD has this been done; a mar - vel in our eyes.
Em7 F♯7 Bm D Em7 ASUS4 A

Psalm 47: God Mounts His Throne

The Ascension of the Lord

Psalm 47:2-3, 6-7, 8-9

Michael Joncas
Tone 1B: Hymn of Praise
from History or Torah

With joy ♩ = 100
Antiphon
Harmony
Melody
God mounts his throne to shouts of joy: a blare of trum - pets, trum - pets for the Lord.
God mounts his throne to shouts of joy: a
God mounts his throne to shouts of joy: a blare of trum - pets, trum - pets for the Lord.
Capo 3: G C A D G C Am7 D DSUS4 D
B♭ E♭ C F B♭ E♭ Cm7 F FSUS4 F

The Ascension of the Lord

Alternate Antiphon
10
Al - le - lu - ia,
Al - le - lu, a - le - lu, al - le - lu - ia
Al - le - lu - ia, al - le - lu - ia,
G C A D
B♭ E♭ C F
14
al - le - lu - ia, al - le - lu - ia.
al - le - lu - ia, al - le - lu - ia.
G C Am7 D DSUS4 D
B♭ E♭ Cm7 F FSUS4 F

The Ascension of the Lord

Verse 1
18
1. All peo - ples, clap your hands. Cry to God with shouts of joy! For the
D C/D Bm D Em D ASUS4 A
F E♭/F Dm F Gm F CSUS4 C
22
LORD, the Most High, is awe - some, the great king o - ver all the earth.
Am Cmaj7 DSUS2 D Am Am7 DSUS4 D
Cm E♭maj7 FSUS2 F Cm Cm7 FSUS4 F
Verse 2
26
2. God has gone up with shouts of joy. The LORD goes up with trum - pet blast. Sing
D C/D Bm D Em D ASUS4 A
F E♭/F Dm F Gm F CSUS4 C

The Ascension of the Lord

30
praise for God; sing praise! Sing praise to our king, sing praise.
Am Cmaj7 DSUS2 D Am Am7 DSUS4 D
Cm Ebmaj7 FSUS2 F Cm Cm7 FSUS4 F
Verse 3
34
3. For God is king of all the earth. Sing praise with a hymn. God is
D C/D Bm D Em D ASUS4 A
F Eb/F Dm F Gm F CSUS4 C
38
reign - ing o - ver na - tions. God sits up - on his ho - ly throne.
Am Cmaj7 DSUS2 D Am Am7 DSUS4 D
Cm Ebmaj7 FSUS2 F Cm Cm7 FSUS4 F

Psalm 103: The Lord Is Kind and Merciful

The Most Sacred Heart of Jesus (Year A)

Psalm 103:1-2, 3-4, 9-10, 11-12

Michael Joncas
Tone 5B: Individual Thanksgiving

Simply ♩ = 85
Antiphon
Harmony
Melody
The Lord's kind - ness is ev - er - last - ing to those who fear him.
D Bm G F♯ Bm F♯m Bm Em ASUS4 A DSUS4 D
Verse 1
1. Bless the LORD, O my soul, and all with - in me, his ho - ly name.
D D/C♯ DSUS2 D Em Dmaj7/C♯ ASUS4 A
Bless the LORD, O my soul, and ne - ver for - get all his be - ne - fits.
Em7 F♯7 Bm D/A Em7 ASUS4 A

The Most Sacred Heart of Jesus (Year A)

Verse 2
2. It is the LORD who for-gives all your sins, who heals ev'-ry one of your ills, who re-
D D/C♯ DSUS2 D Em Dmaj7/C♯ ASUS4 A
deems your life from the grave, who crowns you with mer-cy and com-pas-sion.
Em7 F♯7 Bm D/A Em7 ASUS4 A
Verse 3
3. The LORD does deeds of jus-tice, gives full jus-tice to all who are op-pressed. He made
D D/C♯ DSUS2 D Em Dmaj7/C♯ ASUS4 A

The Most Sacred Heart of Jesus (Year A)

27
known his ways to Mo - ses, and his deeds to the chil-dren of Is - ra - el.
Em7 F♯7 Bm D/A Em7 ASUS4 A
Verse 4
31
4. The LORD is com-pas-sion-ate and gra - cious, slow to an-ger and rich in mer - cy. He does not
D D/C♯ DSUS2 D Em Dmaj7/C♯ ASUS4 A
35
treat us ac - cor - ding to our sins, nor re - pay us ac - cor - ding to our faults.
Em7 F♯7 Bm D/A Em7 ASUS4 A

Psalm 23: The Lord Is My Shepherd

The Most Sacred Heart of Jesus (Year C)

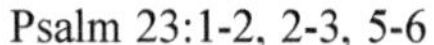

Psalm 23:1-2, 2-3, 5-6

Michael Joncas
Tone 6: Psalm of Confidence

Trustingly ♩ = 80
Antiphon

Harmony
The Lord ___ is my shep - herd; there is no - thing I shall want. ___

Melody
The Lord ___ is my shep - herd; there is no - thing I shall want. ___

Am F C G Am C G7 C

Verse 1

1. The LORD is my shep-herd; there is no-thing I shall want. Fresh and green are the pas - tures where he

Dm7 Am D7 GSUS4 G Am F C G Am

The Most Sacred Heart of Jesus (Year C)

11
gives me re - pose. Near rest - ful wa-ters he leads me; he re-vives my soul.
C Am E7 Am Am/G D GSUS4 G C GSUS4 G
Verse 2
17
2. He guides me a - long the right path, for the sake of his name. Though I should
Dm7 Am D7 GSUS4 G
21
walk in the val - ley of the sha - dow of death, no e - vil would I fear, for
Am F C G Am C Am E7 Am Am/G

The Most Sacred Heart of Jesus (Year C)

25
you are with me. Your crook and your staff will give me com - fort.
D G SUS4 G C G SUS4 G
Verse 3
29
3. You have pre - pared a ta - ble be - fore me in the sight of my foes. My
Dm7 Am D7 G SUS4 G
33
head you have a - noint - ed with oil; my cup is ov - er flow - ing.
Am F C G Am C G SUS4 G

The Most Sacred Heart of Jesus (Year C)

Verse 4
37
4. Sure - ly good-ness and mer-cy shall fol-low me all the days of my life. In the
Dm7
Am
D7
GSUS4
G
41
LORD's own house shall I dwell for length of days un - end - ing.
Am
F
C
G
Am
C
GSUS4
G

Psalm 24: Who Is this King of Glory?

Feast of the Presentation of the Lord

Psalm 24:7, 8, 9, 10

Michael Joncas
Tone 1B: Hymn of Praise
from History or Torah

With exultation ♩ = 90
Antiphon
Harmony
Melody
Who is this king? It is the Lord.
Who is this king of glo - ry? It is the Lord!
Capo 3: G F G C Am7 D GSUS4 G
B♭ A♭ B♭ E♭ Cm7 F B♭SUS4 B♭

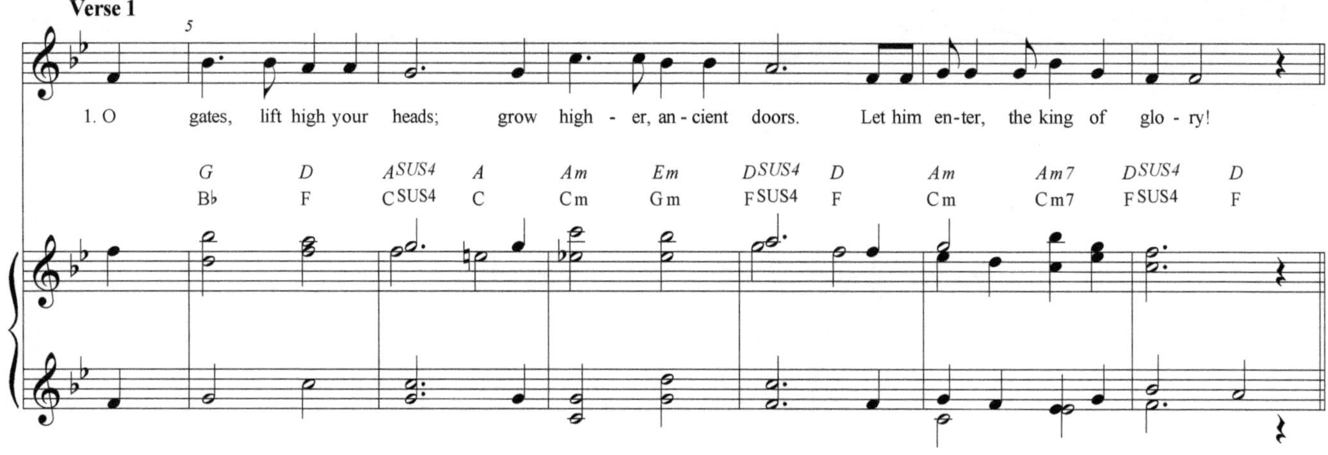

Verse 1
5
1. O gates, lift high your heads; grow high - er, an - cient doors. Let him en-ter, the king of glo - ry!
G D ASUS4 A Am Em DSUS4 D Am Am7 DSUS4 D
B♭ F CSUS4 C Cm Gm FSUS4 F Cm Cm7 FSUS4 F

Feast of the Presentation of the Lord

Verse 2
2. Who is this king of glo - ry? The LORD, the migh-ty, the va-liant; the LORD, va-liant in war.
G D ASUS4 A Am Em DSUS4 D Am Am7 DSUS4 D
B♭ F CSUS4 C Cm Gm FSUS4 F Cm Cm7 FSUS4 F
Verse 3
3. O gates, lift high your heads; grow high - er, an - cient doors. Let him en-ter, the king of glo - ry!
Verse 4
4. Who is this king of glo - ry? He, the LORD of hosts, he is the king of glo - ry!

Psalm 89: The Son of David Will Live For Ever

Solemnity of Saint Joseph, Husband of the Blessed Virgin Mary

Psalm 89:4-5, 16-17, 27, 29

Michael Joncas
Tone 1E: Hymn of Praise to YHWH as King

With confidence ♩ = 90
Antiphon
Harmony
The Son of Da - vid will live, will live for ev - er.
Melody
The Son of Da - vid will live, will live for ev - er.
G D/F♯ Em Am DSUS4 D G
Verse 1
1. I will sing for - ev - er of your mer - cies, O LORD; through all a - ges my mouth will pro -
G Am7/G D/F♯ Em Em7 Am D/C
claim your fi - del - i - ty. I have de - clared your mer - cy is es - tab - lished for - ev - er;
G/B D D7 G C A D

Text: Refrain, *Lectionary for the Mass*, © 1969, 1997, ICEL; Verses, *The Abbey Psalms and Canticles*,

Solemnity of Saint Joseph, Husband of the Blessed Virgin Mary

13
your fi - del - i - ty stands firm as the hea - vens.
D7 Em D G D
Verse 2
17
2. "With my cho-sen one I have made a co - ve - nant; I have sworn to Da - vid my
G Am7/G D/F♯ Em Em7 Am D/C
21
ser - vant: I will es - tab - lish your des - cen-dants for-ev - er,
G/B D D7 G C A D

Solemnity of Saint Joseph, Husband of the Blessed Virgin Mary

25
and set up your throne through all a - ges."
D7 Em D G D
Verse 3
29
3. "He will call out to me, 'You are my fa - ther, my
G Am7/G D/F♯ Em Em7
32
God, the rock of my sal - va - tion.' I will keep my faith - ful
Am D/C G/B D D7 G C
36
love for him al - ways; with him my cov - e - nant shall last."
A D D7 Em D G D

Psalm 40: Here I Am, Lord

Solemnity of the Annunciation of the Lord

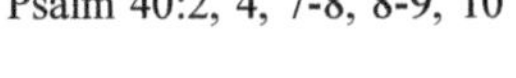

Psalm 40:2, 4, 7-8, 8-9, 10

Michael Joncas
Tone 5B: Individual Thanksgiving

With confidence ♩ = 85
Antiphon
Harmony
Melody
Here am I Lord;
Here I am, I am O Lord, I come to do your will
Here I am, Lord; I come to do your will.
D G D G ASUS4 A7 D

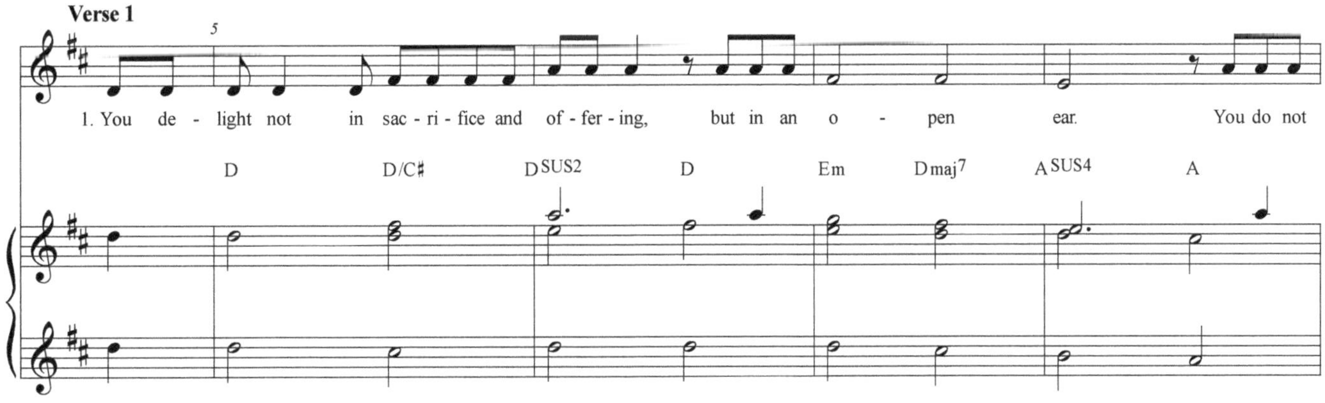
Verse 1
1. You de - light not in sac - ri - fice and of - fer - ing, but in an o - pen ear. You do not
D D/C♯ DSUS2 D Em Dmaj7 ASUS4 A

Solemnity of the Annunciation of the Lord

9
ask for ho - lo - caust and sin of - fer - ing. Then I said, "Be - hold, I have come."
Em7 F♯7 Bm D G6 Em7 ASUS4 A
Verse 2
13
2. In the scroll of the book it stands writ - ten of me: "I de - light to do your will, O my
D D/C♯ DSUS2 D Em Dmaj7
16
God; your in - struc - tion lies deep with - in me."
ASUS4 A G6 Em7 ASUS4 A
Verse 3
19
3. Your up - right-ness I have pro-claimed in the great as - sem - bly.
D D/C♯ DSUS2 D Em Dmaj7 ASUS4

Solemnity of the Annunciation of the Lord

23
My lips I have not sealed; you know it, O LORD.
A Em7 F♯7 Bm D G6 Em7 ASUS4 A
Verse 4
27
4. Your sav-ing help I have not hid-den in my heart; of your faith-ful-ness and sal-va-tion I have
D D/C♯ DSUS2 D Em Dmaj7
30
spo - ken. I made no se-cret of your mer-ci-ful love and your faith-ful-ness to the great as - sem-bly.
ASUS4 A Em7 F♯7 Bm D G6 Em7 ASUS4 A

Psalm 71: Since My Mother's Womb

Solemnity of the Nativity of John the Baptist: Vigil Mass

Psalm 71:1-2, 3-4, 5-6, 15, 17

Michael Joncas
Tone 4B: Individual Lament

With hope ♩ = 90
Antiphon
Harmony
Since my mo-ther's womb, you have been my strength.
Melody
Since my mo - ther's womb, you have been my strength.
Capo 1: Am D Am7 D EmSUS4 Em
B♭m E♭ B♭m7 E♭ FmSUS4 Fm
Verse 1
5
1. In you, O Lord, I take re - fuge; let me ne - ver be put to shame. In your up -
Em7 Am/G Em7 AmSUS2 Em7 AmSUS2
Fm7 B♭m/A♭ Fm7 B♭mSUS2 Fm7 B♭mSUS2
9
right - ness, res - cue me, free me; in - cline your ear to me and save me.
Cmaj7 AmSUS6 Cmaj7 D6 EmSUS4 Em/B B
D♭maj7 B♭mSUS6 D♭maj7 E♭6 FmSUS4 Fm/C C

Solemnity of the Nativity of John the Baptist: Vigil Mass

Verse 2
13
2. Be my rock, my con - stant re - fuge, a migh - ty strong - hold to save me, for
Em7 Am/G Em7 AmSUS2 Em7 AmSUS2
Fm7 B♭m/A♭ Fm7 B♭mSUS2 Fm7 B♭mSUS2
17
3
you are my rock, my strong - hold. My God, free me from the hand of the wic - ked.
Cmaj7 AmSUS6 Cmaj7 D6 EmSUS4 Em/B B
D♭maj7 B♭mSUS6 D♭maj7 E♭6 FmSUS4 Fm/C C
Verse 3
21
3. It is you, O LORD, who are my hope, my trust, O LORD, from my youth. On
Em7 Am/G Em7 AmSUS2 Em7 AmSUS2
Fm7 B♭m/A♭ Fm7 B♭mSUS2 Fm7 B♭mSUS2

Solemnity of the Nativity of John the Baptist: Vigil Mass

25
you I have leaned from my birth; from my mo-ther's womb, you have drawn me forth.
Cmaj7 AmSUS6 Cmaj7 D6 EmSUS4 Em/B B
D♭maj7 B♭mSUS6 D♭maj7 E♭6 FmSUS4 Fm/C C
Verse 4
29
4. My mouth will tell of your jus - tice, and all the day long of your sal - va - tion. O
3
Em7 Am/G Em7 AmSUS2 Em7 AmSUS2
Fm7 B♭m/A♭ Fm7 B♭mSUS2 Fm7 B♭mSUS2
33
God, you have taught me from my youth, and I pro - claim your won - ders still.
Cmaj7 AmSUS6 Cmaj7 D6 EmSUS4 Em/B B
D♭maj7 B♭mSUS6 D♭maj7 E♭6 FmSUS4 Fm/C C

Psalm 139: I Praise You

Solemnity of the Nativity of John the Baptist: Mass during the Day

Psalm 139:1-3, 13-14, 14-15

Michael Joncas
Tone 4B: Individual Lament

With hope ♩ = 90
Antiphon
Harmony
I praise you, for I am won - der - f'ly made.
Melody
I praise you, for I am won - der-f'ly made.
Capo 1: Am D Am7 D EmSUS4 Em
B♭m E♭ B♭m7 E♭ FmSUS4 Fm
Verse 1
1. O Lord, you search me and you know me. You your - self know my rest - ing and my
Em7 Am/G Em7 AmSUS2 Em7
Fm7 B♭m/A♭ Fm7 B♭mSUS2 Fm7

Solemnity of the Nativity of John the Baptist: Mass during the Day

8
ris - ing; you dis - cern my thoughts from a - far. You mark when I walk or lie
AmSUS2 Cmaj7 AmSUS6 Cmaj7 Em Am
B♭mSUS2 D♭maj7 B♭mSUS6 D♭maj7 Fm B♭m
12
down; you know all my ways through and through.
D D6 EmSUS4 Em/B B
E♭ E♭6 FmSUS4 Fm/C C
Verse 2
15
2. For it was you who formed my in - most be - ing, knit me to - ge - ther in my mo - ther's
Em7 Am/G Em7 AmSUS2 Em7
Fm7 B♭m/A♭ Fm7 B♭mSUS2 Fm7

Solemnity of the Nativity of John the Baptist: Mass during the Day

18
womb. I thank you who won-der-ful-ly made me; how won-der-ful are your works.
AmSUS2 Cmaj7 AmSUS6 Cmaj7 D6 EmSUS4 Em/B B
B♭mSUS2 D♭maj7 B♭mSUS6 D♭maj7 E♭6 FmSUS4 Fm/C C
Verse 3
23
3. My soul knows them well! My frame was not hid-den from you, when
Em7 Am/G Em7 AmSUS2 Em7 AmSUS2
Fm7 B♭m/A♭ Fm7 B♭mSUS2 Fm7 B♭mSUS2
27
I was be-ing fa-shioned in se-cret and mol-ded in the depths of the earth.
Cmaj7 AmSUS6 Cmaj7 D6 EmSUS4 Em/B B
D♭maj7 B♭mSUS6 D♭maj7 E♭6 FmSUS4 Fm/C C

Psalm 19: Their Message Goes Out

Solemnity of Saints Peter and Paul, Apostles: Vigil Mass

Psalm 19:2-3, 4-5

Michael Joncas
Tone 1A: Hymn of Praise
Motivation from Nature

With awe ♩ = 80
Antiphon
Harmony
Their mes - sage goes out through all the earth.
Melody
Their mes - sage goes out through all the earth.
F G C Dm7 G C
Verse 1
1. The hea - vens de-clare the glo - ry of God, and the fir - ma - ment pro-claims the work of his hands.
C G Am C/G Dm7 Dm GSUS4 G
Day un - to day breathes forth a word, and night un - to night im-parts the know - ledge.
A A7 DmSUS2 Dm C GSUS4 G

Solemnity of Saints Peter and Paul, Apostles: Vigil Mass

Verse 2
12
2. No speech, no word, whose voice goes un - heed - ed; their sound goes forth through all the
C G/B Am C/G Dm7 Dm
15
earth, their mes - sage to the ut - most bounds of the world.
GSUS4 G C GSUS4 G

Psalm 34: The Angel of the Lord

Solemnity of Saints Peter and Paul, Apostles: Mass during the Day

Psalm 34:2-3, 4-5, 6-7, 8-9

Michael Joncas
Tone 8A: Wisdom Psalm

With delight ♩ = 80
Antiphon
Harmony
The an - gel of the Lord will res - cue those who fear him.
Melody
The an - gel of the Lord will res - cue those who fear him.
D F♯m Em7 A7 DSUS4 D
Verse 1
1. I will bless the LORD at all times, praise of him is al-ways in my mouth. In the
D A Bm D/A Em7 D A A7
LORD my soul shall make its boast; the hum-ble shall hear and be glad.
D G Bm Bm/A E7 ASUS4 A

Solemnity of Saints Peter and Paul, Apostles: Mass during the Day

Verse 2
2. Glo - ri - fy the LORD with me, to - ge - ther let us praise his name. I
D A Bm D/A Em7 D A A7
sought the LORD, and he an - swered me; from all my ter - rors he set me free.
D G Bm Bm/A E7 ASUS4 A
Verse 3
3. Look t'ward him and be ra - diant; let your fa - ces not be a - bashed. This
D A Bm D/A Em7 D A A7

Solemnity of Saints Peter and Paul, Apostles: Mass during the Day

25
low - ly one called; the LORD heard, and res-cued him from all his dis - tress.
D G Bm Bm/A E7 ASUS4 A
Verse 4
29
4. The an - gel of the LORD is en-camped a-round those who fear him, to res-cue them.
D A Bm D/A Em7 D A A7
33
Taste and see that the LORD is good. Bless-ed the man who seeks re-fuge in him.
D G Bm Bm/A E7 ASUS4 A

Psalm 100: We Are His People

Independence Day

Psalm 100:1-2, 3, 5

Michael Joncas
Tone 1D: Processional

March-like ♩ = 100
Antiphon
Harmony
We are his peo - ple: the sheep of his flock, the sheep of his flock.
Melody
We are his peo - ple: the sheep of his flock, the sheep of his flock.
C F Dm GSUS4 G Am Dm F G7 C
Verse 1
1. Cry out with joy to the LORD, all the earth. Serve the LORD with glad - ness. Come be-
Cmaj7 F C GSUS4 G F G CSUS4 C
fore him, sing - ing for joy. Come be - fore him, sing - ing for joy.
F E7 Am F C GSUS4 G

Independence Day

Verse 2
2. Know that he, the Lord, is God. He made us; we be-long to him. We are his
Cmaj7 F C GSUS4 G F G CSUS4 C
peo-ple, the sheep of his flock; his peo ple, the sheep of his flock.
F E7 Am F C GSUS4 G
Verse 3
3. In - deed, how good is the Lord, e - ter - nal his mer-ci-ful love. He is
Cmaj7 F C GSUS4 G F G CSUS4 C
faith-ful from age to age; He is faith-ful from age to age.
F E7 Am F C GSUS4 G

Psalm 97: The Lord Is King

Feast of the Transfiguration of the Lord

Psalm 97:1-2, 5-6, 9

Michael Joncas
Tone 1E: Hymn of Praise to YHWH as King

With confidence ♩ = 85
Antiphon
Harmony
The Lord is king, the Lord is king, the Most High o - ver all the earth.
Melody
The Lord is king, the Lord is king, the Most High o - ver all the earth.
G D/F♯ Em Am DSUS4 D G
Verse 1
1. The LORD is king, let earth re - joice; let the ma - ny is-lands be glad.
G Am/G D Em Em7 Am D/C G/B D D7
Cloud and dark-ness sur - round him; jus - tice and right are the foun - da - tion of his throne.
G C A D D7 Em D/C G/B D

Feast of the Transfiguration of the Lord

Verse 2
18
2. The moun - tains melt like wax be - fore the face of the LORD, be - fore the face of the LORD of
G Am/G D Em Em7 Am D/C
22
all the earth. The skies pro - claim his jus - tice;
G/B D D7 G C A D
26
all peo - ples see his glo - ry.
D7 Em D/C G/B D

Feast of the Transfiguration of the Lord

Verse 3
30
3. For you in - deed are the LORD, most high a-bove
G Am/G D Em Em7 G C
34
all the earth, ex - alt - ed far a - bove all gods.
A D D7 Em D/C G/B D

Psalm 132: Lord, Go Up to the Place of Your Rest

Solemnity of the Assumption of the Blessed Virgin Mary: Vigil Mass

Psalm 132:6-7, 9-10, 13-14

Michael Joncas
Tone 1D: Processional

March-like ♩ = 80
Antiphon
Harmony
Lord, go up to the place of your rest, you and the ark of your ho - li - ness.
Melody
Lord, go up to the place of your rest, you and the ark of your ho - li - ness.
C Dm B♭ F C Dm G C
Verse 1
1. We heard of it at Eph - ra - ta; we found it in the plains of Yea-rim: "Let us
Cmaj7 Dm7 GSUS4 G F G CSUS4 C
go to the place of his dwell - ing; let us bow down at his foot - stool."
F E7 Am C D7 GSUS4 G

Verse 2
14
2. Your priests shall be clothed with jus - tice; your faith-ful shall ring out their joy. For the
Cmaj7 Dm7 GSUS4 G F G CSUS4 C
18
sake of Da - vid your ser - vant, do not re - ject your a - noint - ed.
3
F E7 Am C D7 GSUS4 G
Verse 3
22
3. For the LORD has cho - sen Zi - on; he has de - sired it for his dwell - ing:
Cmaj7 Dm7 GSUS4 G F G CSUS4 C
26
"This is my rest - ing place from age to age; here have I de - sired to dwell."
F E7 Am C D7 GSUS4 G

Psalm 45: The Queen Stands

Solemnity of the Assumption of the Blessed Virgin Mary: Mass during the Day

Psalm 45:10, 11, 12, 16
Michael Joncas
Tone 2D: Royal Davidic Marriage
With strength ♩ = 110
Antiphon
Harmony
Melody
The queen stands at your right hand, arrayed in gold.
ar - rayed in gold.
E E7 Am E
Verse 1
1. On your right stands the queen, stands the queen in gold of O - phir.
E Am E7 E Am F E Am
Verse 2
2. Lis - ten, O daugh-ter; pay heed and give ear: for - get your own peo - ple and your fa - ther's house.
E Am E7 E Am F E Am

Solemnity of the Assumption of the Blessed Virgin Mary: Mass during the Day

21
Verse 3
3. So will the king de - sire your beau-ty. He is your lord, pay ho-mage to him.
E Am E7 E Am F E Am
29
Verse 4
4. They are es - cort-ed a-mid glad-ness and joy; they pass with-in the pa-lace, the pa-lace of the king.
3
E Am E7 E Am F E Am

Psalm 78: Do Not Forget the Works of the Lord

Feast of the Exaltation of the Holy Cross

Psalm 78:1-2, 34-35, 36-37, 38
Michael Joncas
Tone 1B: Hymn of Praise from History or Torah
Like a ballad ♩ = 80
Antiphon
Harmony
Melody
Do not for-get the works of the Lord! Do not for-get the works of the Lord!
Capo 3:
Verse 1
1. Give ear, my peo-ple, to my teach - ing; in-cline your ear to the words of my mouth. I will
o - pen my mouth in a pa-ra-ble and ut - ter hid - den les - sons of the past.

Feast of the Exaltation of the Holy Cross

Verse 2
2. When he slew them, then they sought him, re - pent-ed and ear-nest-ly sought God. They would re-
D C/D Bm D Em D ASUS4 A
F Eb/F Dm F Gm F CSUS4 C
mem - ber that God was their rock, God the Most High their re - deem - er.
Am Cmaj7 DSUS4 D Am7 DSUS4 D
Cm Ebmaj7 FSUS4 F Cm7 FSUS4 F
Verse 3
3. Yet they de - ceived him with their mouths; they lied to him with their tongues. For their
D C/D Bm D Em D ASUS4 A
F Eb/F Dm F Gm F CSUS4 C

Feast of the Exaltation of the Holy Cross

25
hearts were not stead - fast toward him; they were not faith - ful to his cov-e-nant.
Am Cmaj7 DSUS4 D Am7 DSUS4 D
Cm E♭maj7 FSUS4 F Cm7 FSUS4 F
Verse 4
29
4. Yet he who is full of com - pas - sion for - gave them their sin and spared them. So
D C/D Bm D Em D ASUS4 A
F E♭/F Dm F Gm F CSUS4 C
33
of - ten he held back his an - ger, and did not stir up all his rage.
Am Cmaj7 DSUS4 D Am7 DSUS4 D
Cm E♭maj7 FSUS4 F Cm7 FSUS4 F

Psalm 24: Lord, This Is the People

Solemnity of All Saints

Psalm 24:1-2, 3-4, 5-6

Michael Joncas
Tone 1D: Processional

With strength ♩ = 80
Antiphon
Harmony
Lord, this is the peo - ple that longs to see your face.
Melody
Lord, this is the peo - ple that longs to see your face.
Am F Em7 Am Dm7 G CSUS4 C
Verse 1
1. The LORD's is the earth and its full - ness; the world, and those who dwell in it.
Cmaj7 F C GSUS4 G F C CSUS4 C
It is he who set it on the seas; on the ri - vers he made it firm.
C F E7 Am F C GSUS4 G

Solemnity of All Saints

13
Verse 2
2. Who shall climb the moun - tain of the LORD? Who shall stand in his ho - ly place?
Cmaj7 F C GSUS4 G F C CSUS4 C
17
The clean of hands and pure of heart, whose soul is not set on vain things.
3
F E7 Am F C GSUS4 G
21
Verse 3
3. Bless - ings from the LORD shall he re - ceive, and right re - ward from the God who saves him.
Cmaj7 F C GSUS4 G F C CSUS4 C
25
Such are the peo - ple who seek him, who seek the face of the God of Ja - cob.
F E7 Am F C

Psalm 23: The Lord Is My Shepherd

The Commemoration of All the Faithful Departed (All Souls) 1

Psalm 23:1-2, 2-3, 5-6

Michael Joncas
Tone 6: Psalm of Confidence

Trustingly ♩ = 80
Antiphon
Harmony
The Lord is my shep - herd; there is no - thing I shall want.
Melody
The Lord is my shep - herd; there is no - thing I shall want.
Am F C G Am C G7 C
Alternate Antiphon
5
Walk in dark - ness; you are with me.
Though I walk in the val - ley of dark - ness, I fear no e - vil for you are with me.
C G/B Am Em/G Dm F G CSUS4 C

Verse 1
1. The Lord is my shep-herd; there is no-thing I shall want. Fresh and green are the pas - tures where he
Dm7 Am D7 GSUS4 G Am F C G Am
gives me re - pose. Near rest - ful wa-ters he leads me; he re-vives my soul.
C Am E7 Am Am/G D GSUS4 G C GSUS4 G
Verse 2
2. He guides me a - long the right path, for the sake of his name. Though I should
Dm7 Am D7 GSUS4 G

The Commemoration of All the Faithful Departed (All Souls) 1

23
walk in the val - ley of the sha - dow of death, no e - vil would I fear, for
Am F C G Am G Am E7 Am Am/G
27
you are with me. Your crook and your staff will give me com - fort.
D GSUS4 G C GSUS4 G
Verse 3
31
3
3. You have pre - pared a ta - ble be - fore me in the sight of my foes. My
Dm7 Am D7 GSUS4 G

35
head you have a - noint - ed with oil; my cup is ov - er - flow - ing.
Am F C G Am C GSUS4 G
39
Verse 4
4. Sure - ly good - ness and mer - cy shall fol - low me all the days of my life. In the
Dm7 Am D7 GSUS4 G
44
Lord's own house shall I dwell for length of days un - end - ing.
Am F C G Am C GSUS4 G

Psalm 25: To You, O Lord

The Commemoration of All the Faithful Departed (All Souls) 2

Psalm 25:6 and 7b, 17-18, 20-21 (1) (3a)

Michael Joncas
Tone 8B: Wisdom Psalm

Simply ♩ = 80
Antiphon
Harmony
To you, O Lord, to you, O Lord, I lift, lift my soul.
Melody
To you, O Lord, to you, O Lord, I lift, I lift my soul.
Capo 1: G A7 D Em A DSUS4 D
A♭ B♭7 E♭ Fm B♭ E♭SUS4 E♭

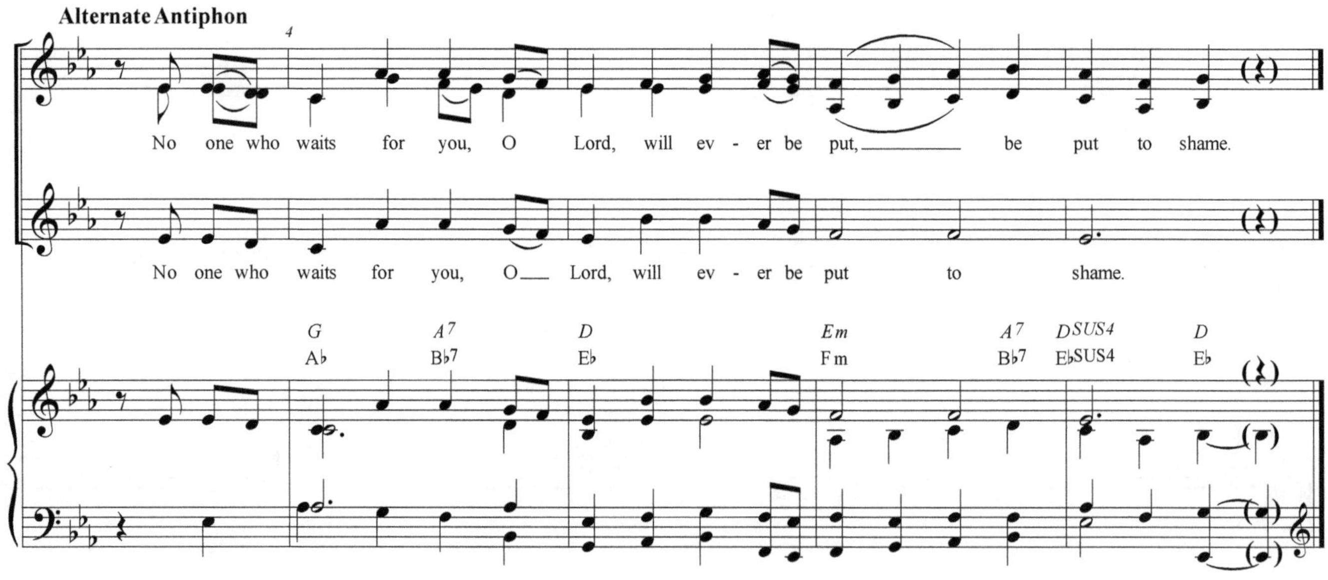

Alternate Antiphon
No one who waits for you, O Lord, will ev - er be put, be put to shame.
No one who waits for you, O Lord, will ev - er be put to shame.
G A7 D Em A7 DSUS4 D
A♭ B♭7 E♭ Fm B♭7 E♭SUS4 E♭

The Commemoration of All the Faithful Departed (All Souls) 2

Verse 1
1. Re - mem-ber your com-pas - sion, O Lord, and your mer - ci - ful love, for they are from of old.
D6 Gmaj7 Em7 A Dmaj7 E ASUS4 A7
E♭6 A♭maj7 Fm7 B♭ E♭maj7 F B♭SUS4 B♭7
In your mer - ci - ful love re - mem-ber me, be - cause of your good - ness, O Lord.
Bm F♯m/A Gmaj7 A7/G Dmaj7 G ASUS4 A
Cm Gm/B♭ A♭maj7 B♭7/A♭ E♭maj7 A♭ B♭SUS4 B♭
Verse 2
2. Re - lieve the an-guish of my heart, and set me free from my dis - tress.
D6 Gmaj7 Em7 A Dmaj7 E ASUS4 A7
E♭6 A♭maj7 Fm7 B♭ E♭maj7 F B♭SUS4 B♭7

The Commemoration of All the Faithful Departed (All Souls) 2

21
See my low - li - ness and suf - fer - ing, and take a - way all my sins.
Bm F♯m/A Gmaj7 A7/G Dmaj7 G ASUS4 A7
Cm Gm/B♭ A♭maj7 B♭7/A♭ E♭maj7 A♭ B♭SUS4 B♭7
Verse 3
25
3. Pre - serve my life, and res - cue me. Let me not be put to shame, for in you I take re - fuge.
D6 Gmaj7 Em7 A Dmaj7 E ASUS4 A7/G
E♭6 A♭maj7 Fm7 B♭ E♭maj7 F B♭SUS4 B♭7/A♭
29
May in - te - gri - ty and vir - tue pro - tect me, for I have hoped in you, O LORD.
Bm F♯m/A Gmaj7 A7/G Dmaj7 G ASUS4 A
Cm Gm/B♭ A♭maj7 B♭7/A♭ E♭maj7 A♭ B♭SUS4 B♭

Psalm 27: The Lord Is My Light

The Commemoration of All the Faithful Departed (All Souls) 3

Psalm 27:1, 4, 7 and 8b and 9a, 13-14

Michael Joncas
Tone 6: Psalm of Confidence

With confidence ♩ = 90

Antiphon

Harmony

The Lord ___ is my light and my sal - va - tion.

Melody

The Lord ___ is my light and my sal - va - tion.

Am F G F Dm C G C

Alternate Antiphon

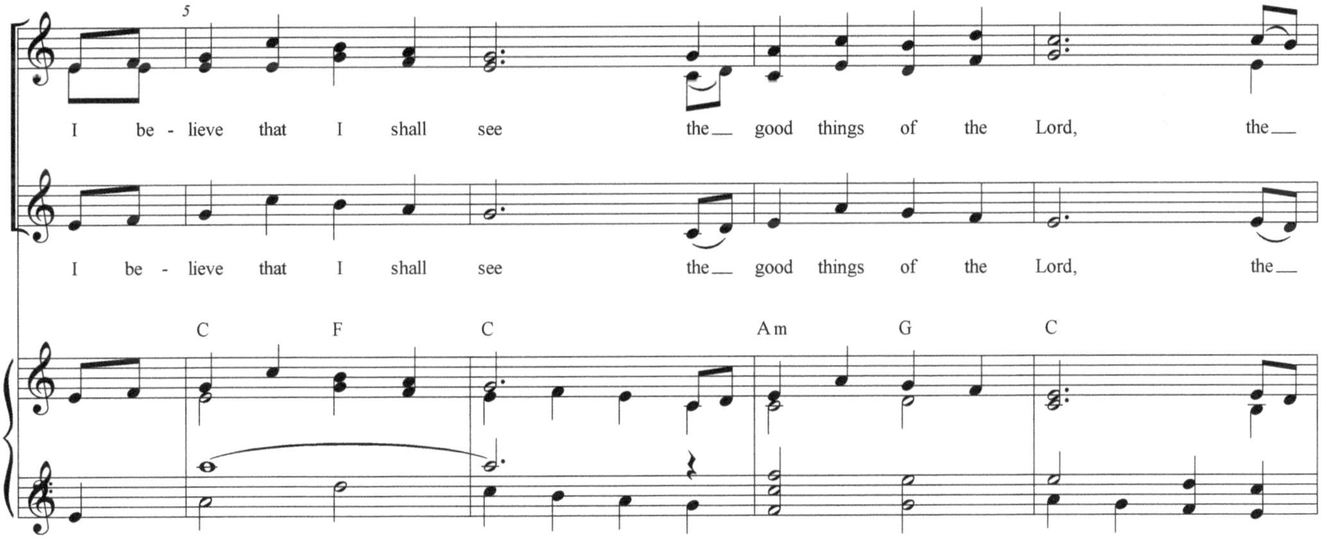

5

I be - lieve that I shall see the ___ good things of the Lord, the ___

I be - lieve that I shall see the ___ good things of the Lord, the ___

C F C Am G C

The Commemoration of All the Faithful Departed (All Souls) 3

9
good things of the Lord in the land of the liv - ing.
good things of the Lord in the land of the liv - ing.
F C/G C/E Am Dm G7 C
Verse 1
13
1. The LORD is my light and my sal - va - tion; whom shall I fear? The
Dm7 Am D7 GSUS4 G
17
LORD is the strong-hold of my life; whom should I dread?
Am F C G Am C GSUS4 G

Verse 2
21
2. There is one thing I ask of the LORD, on - ly this do I seek: to
Dm7 Am D7 G SUS4 G
25
live in the house of the LORD all the days of my life, to
Am F C G Am C Am E Am Am7/G
29
gaze on the beau - ty of the LORD, to in - quire at his tem - ple.
D G SUS4 G C G SUS4 G

The Commemoration of All the Faithful Departed (All Souls) 3

Verse 3
3. O LORD, hear my voice when I call; have mer - cy and an-swer me. It is your
Dm7 Am D7 GSUS4 G
face, O LORD, that I seek hide not your face from me.
Am F C G Am C GSUS4 G
Verse 4
4. I be - lieve I shall see the LORD's good - ness in the land of the liv - ing.
Dm7 Am D7 GSUS4 G

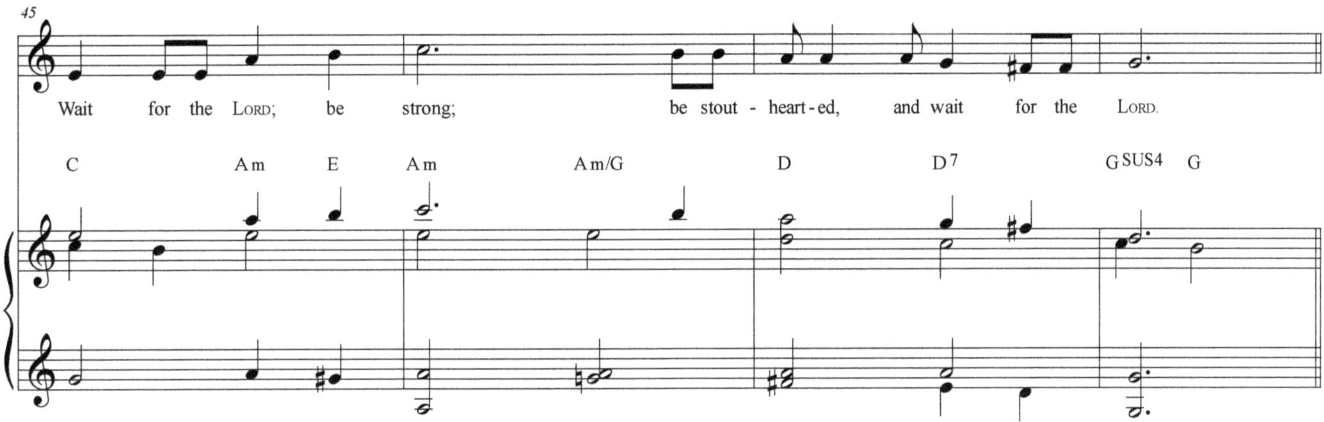
45
Wait for the LORD; be strong; be stout - heart-ed, and wait for the LORD.
C Am E Am Am/G D D7 GSUS4 G

Psalm 46: The Waters of the River

Feast of the Dedication of the Lateran Basilica in Rome

Psalm 46:2-3, 5-6, 8-9
Michael Joncas
Tone 1C: Song of Zion
Flowing ♩ = 80
Antiphon
Harmony
Melody
The waters of the river gladden the city of God, the holy dwelling of the Most High!
Capo 2: D G/D Dmaj7 D D/F♯ G Em A D
E A/E Emaj7 E E/G♯ A F♯m B E
Verse 1
1. God is for us a refuge and strength, an ever present help in time of distress: so we shall not fear though the earth should rock, though the mountains quake to the heart of the sea.
D Em A A7 DSUS4 D G
E F♯m B B7 ESUS4 E A
F♯m D/F♯ Em F♯7 Bm G D/F♯ Em A Bm7 G ASUS4 A
G♯m E/G♯ F♯m G♯7 C♯m A E/G♯ F♯m B C♯m7 A BSUS4 B

Feast of the Dedication of the Lateran Basilica in Rome

Verse 2
18
2. The waters of a river give joy to God's city, the holy place, the abode of the Most High.
D Em A A7 DSUS4 D
E F♯m B B7 ESUS4 E
22
God is in her midst; she cannot be shaken;
G F♯m D/F♯ Em F♯7 Bm
A G♯m E/G♯ F♯m G♯7 C♯m
26
God will help her at the dawning of the day.
G D/F♯ Em A Bm7 G ASUS4 A
A E/G♯ F♯m B C♯m7 A BSUS4 B

Feast of the Dedication of the Lateran Basilica in Rome

Verse 3
30
3. The LORD of hosts is with us; the God of Ja-cob is our strong - hold. Come and be -
D E
Em F♯m
A B
A7 B7
Bm C♯m
34
hold the works of the LORD, the awe-some deeds he has done on the earth.
3
G A
D/F♯ E/G♯
Em F♯m
A B
Bm7 C♯m7
G A
ASUS4 A
BSUS4 B

1 Chronicles 29: We Praise Your Glorious Name*

Thanksgiving Day

1 Chronicles 29:10bc, 11, 12

Michael Joncas
Tone 1A: Hymn of Praise
Motivation from Nature

With exaltation ♩ = 85
Antiphon
Harmony
Melody
praise your
We praise your glo - rious name, O migh - ty God.
We praise your glo-ri-ous name, O migh - ty God.
C Am Em Am F Dm7 G CSUS4 C
Verse 1
1. Bless-ed are you, O LORD, God of Is - ra - el, our fa - ther, from e - ter-ni-ty un-to e - ter - ni - ty.
C G/B Am Am/G Dm Dm7 GSUS4 G C GSUS4 G
Verse 2
2. Yours, O LORD, is great-ness and power, splen - dor, vic-t'ry and ma-jes-ty; for all is yours in hea-ven and on
C G/B Am Am/G Dm Dm7 GSUS4 G Am Am/G

*This psalm is one of several options from the Lectionary.

Thanksgiving Day

16
earth. Yours, O Lord, is the king - dom, you are ex - alt - ed as head o - ver all.
D G F C G C GSUS4 G
21 Verse 3
3. Rich - es and ho - nor are from you, and you have do - mi - nion o - ver all. In your
C G/B Am Am/G Dm Dm7 GSUS4 G
25
hand is power and might; your hand gives great-ness and strength to all.
G F D C G GSUS4 C

Psalm 98: Sing to the Lord a New Song

Solemnity of the Immaculate Conception of the Blessed Virgin Mary

Psalm 98:1, 2-3, 3-4

Michael Joncas
Tone 1E: Hymn of Praise
to YHWH as King

With exultation ♩. = 50
Antiphon
Harmony
Sing to the Lord a new song, for he has done mar - ve-lous deeds.
Melody
Sing to the Lord a new song, for he has done mar - ve-lous deeds.
Capo 2: D G6/D Gm/D D D/F♯ G A7 D
E A6/E Am/E E E/G♯ A B7 E
Verse 1
1. O sing a new song to the LORD, for he has worked won - ders. His
D Em/D Gm/D D D/F♯ E7 A A7
E F♯m/E Am/E E E/G♯ F♯7 B B7

Solemnity of the Immaculate Conception of the Blessed Virgin Mary

9
right hand and his ho - ly arm have brought sal - va - tion.
D Em/D Gm/D D Bm Em A A7
E F♯m/E Am/E E C♯m F♯m B B7
Verse 2
13
2. The LORD has made known his sal - va - tion, has shown his de - liv' - rance to the na -
D Em/D Gm/D D F♯m/A Bm D/F♯ E7
E F♯m/E Am/E E G♯m/B C♯m E/G♯ F♯7
17
tions. He has re - mem - bered his mer - ci - ful love and his truth for the house of Is - ra - el.
A A7 D Em/D Gm/D D Bm Em A A7
B B7 E F♯m/E Am/E E C♯m F♯m B B7

Solemnity of the Immaculate Conception of the Blessed Virgin Mary

Verse 3
3. All the ends of the earth have seen the sal - va - tion by our God. Shout to the
D Em/D Gm/D D D/F♯ E7 A A7
E F♯m/E Am/E E E/G♯ F♯7 B B7
LORD, all the earth; break forth in - to joy - ous song and sing out your praise.
D Em/D Gm/D D Bm Em A A7
E F♯m/E Am/E E C♯m F♯m B B7

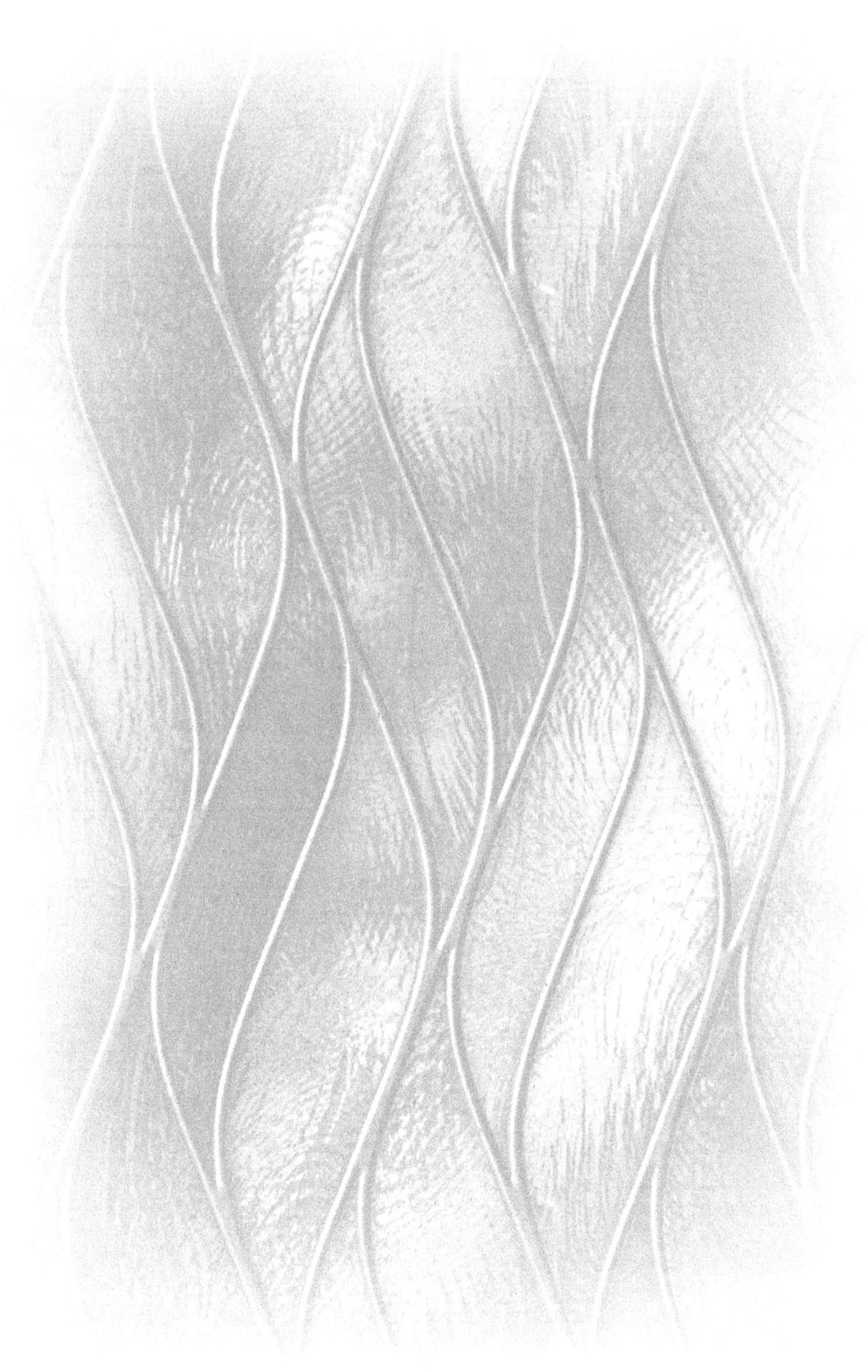

Judith 13: You Are the Highest Honor

Feast of Our Lady of Guadalupe

Judith 13:18bcde, 19
Michael Joncas
Flowing ♩ = 80
Antiphon
You are the high - est ho - nor of our race, the high - est ho - nor of our race.
You are the high - est ho - nor of our race, the high - est ho - nor of our race.
C F/A C/G F G7 Am Dm7/F C/G F/A G CSUS4 C
Verse 1
1. Bless-ed are you, O daugh-ter, by God Most High; you are a - bove all wo-men on earth, and
C B♭ F C Em Dm/F C/G G
bless - ed be the Lord God, who has cre - a - ted the hea-vens and the earth.
C B♭ F Am Em D GSUS4 G

Feast of Our Lady of Guadalupe

Verse 2
13
2. For your deed of hope will ne - ver de - part, your deed of hope will ne - ver de - part from the
C Bb F C Em Dm/F C/G G
17
hearts of those who al - ways re - mem - ber, re - mem - ber the power of God.
C Bb F Am Em D GSUS4 G